D0948714

NATURALIZING PHILOSOPHY
OF EDUCATION

NATURALIZING PHILOSOPHY OF EDUCATION

JOHN DEWEY IN THE POSTANALYTIC PERIOD

JEROME A. POPP

SOUTHERN ILLINOIS UNIVERSITY PRESS

CARBONDALE AND EDWARDSVILLE

Library of Congress Cataloging-in-Publication Data

Popp, Jerome A., 1938–
 Naturalizing philosophy of education : John Dewey in the
postanalytic period / Jerome A. Popp.
  p. cm.
 Includes bibliographical references (p.) and index.
 1. Dewey, John, 1859–1952. 2. Education—Philosophy. I. Title.
LB875.D5P67   1998
370′.1—dc21   97-38677
 ISBN 0-8093-2171-8 (cloth : alk. paper)   CIP

Extract from McCauley, Robert E., "Epistemology in an Age of Cognitive Science,"
Philosophical Psychology vol. 1, no. 2 (1988): pp. 143–52, reprinted by permission of the
publisher, Carfax Publishing Limited, PO Box 25, Abingdon, Oxfordshire OX14 3UE,
United Kingdom.

Extracts from R. N. Giere, "Philosophy of Science Naturalized," *Philosophy of Science* 52
(Sept. 1985): 331–56, copyright © 1985 by the Philosophy of Science Association. Reprinted
by permission of the publisher, the University of Chicago Press.

TO THE MEMORY
OF PROFESSOR PHILIP G. SMITH

CONTENTS

PREFACE

As a student of Philip G. Smith, Wesley Salmon, and Ronald Giere at Indiana University, I spent much time trying to understand how Dewey's ideas were related to the arguments I was encountering in the philosophy of science literature. The field of philosophy of education at that time seemed to have two centers of energy: language analysis and Marxism. Both believed the tradition created by Dewey's writings required revision, and neither seemed to address the arguments I had been studying.

At the same time that criticism of empiricism was growing in philosophy of science and epistemology, philosophic problems in cognitive science began to receive increased attention. This required a rethinking of the relationship between philosophy and psychology and a reevaluation of the arguments presented by the pragmatists. In philosophy of education, studies in language analysis decreased markedly, but there was little concomitant interest in the developments occurring in epistemology and philosophy of science.

The goal of this book is to rekindle an interest in epistemological issues within philosophy of education and to show that Dewey's arguments are related to contemporary concerns. This discussion is important to educators for at least two reasons: (a) the methodology of conceptual analysis is as important today as it ever was, but it must be reconstructed in light of the criticisms of empiricism and the positive arguments presented by the naturalists; (b) the view of education presented by Dewey is legitimated by his epistemological arguments. If these arguments are misunderstood or ignored, then Dewey's view of education can be distorted to justify practices that are actually unacceptable to Dewey's approach (I believe this is now happening). An adequate evaluation of what Dewey's approach means for education requires a consideration of his arguments in light of contemporary thought.

I want to thank professors Dave Denton, Dave Owen, Mike Oliker, and Ron

Swartz for their comments on early versions of this project and for their support and encouragement for my completing it. I am especially grateful to Philip G. Smith, Philip L. Smith, and Marcia S. Popp, three professors whose enthusiasm for talking about Dewey invigorated my thinking and increased my understanding of the topics considered in this book.

NATURALIZING PHILOSOPHY
OF EDUCATION

1

THE REEMERGENCE OF PRAGMATISM

Introduction

MANY AMERICAN PHILOSOPHERS are enthusiastically reconsidering John Dewey's ideas, partly because of the recent publication of his collected works, but, more important, because of the widely recognized failure of empiricism to achieve its philosophic objectives. The pragmatism Dewey articulated is of interest to many because it has long been an alternative to empiricism. This enthusiasm, however, has not yet spilled over into philosophy of education, the natural home for Dewey's ideas. The underappreciation of the philosophic significance of Dewey's arguments and how they are being extended today indicates serious deficiencies within contemporary philosophy of education, both as a field of inquiry and as a component within teacher and administrator education programs.

Dewey attempted to improve educational thought and practice by articulating an adequate philosophic view in light of which both could benefit. Some of his efforts were aimed at making educational thought and practice more coherent, whereas others were focused on evaluating attempts to direct educational practice through the invocation of various philosophic points of view. Today's educators still receive advice about the proper policies for schools from people who embrace particular metaphysical doctrines, but they are also confronted with the findings of various studies collected under the rubric "cognitive science" (artificial intelligence, linguistics, neuroscience, cognitive psychology, theory of mind, philosophy of science, and epistemology).[1] As such studies continue to develop, more and more proposals for the improvement of education may well emerge.

One might expect that this sort of thinking would be welcome grist for the mill in philosophy of education, but there is actually very little attention being paid to these inquiries and what they mean for education. In what follows, I will show why Dewey's arguments present viable solutions to issues that must be addressed in any serious attempt to develop an adequate philosophic view of educational thought and practice. (Much of what is currently being presented as discourse in educational foundations is without much philosophic warrant, and thereby miseducative in its own right.) This quest is an attempt to convey what Dewey's pragmatism offers philosophy of education and actual classroom practice.

The Rise and Fall of Empiricism in Philosophy of Education

An understanding of contemporary pragmatism is in many ways dependent on an appreciation of the reasons for the rise and fall of empiricism in twentieth-century philosophy and philosophy of education. During the early years of the twentieth century, John Dewey's pragmatic (or naturalistic) view was virtually the establishment theory, or the "received" view, in philosophy of education, although this does not mean that very many of the schools of this period actually operated on Dewey's ideas or principles.

But by midcentury pragmatism was being supplanted by empiricism. How was empiricism able to replace Dewey's well-established ideas as the logical or cognitive center of philosophy of education? And why is it that the arguments of the pragmatists are now supplanting empiricism, twenty-five years after empiricism's domination of the discourse in philosophy of education? How we interpret the successes and failures of twentieth-century empiricism will influence how we evaluate both Dewey's pragmatism and the worth of philosophy of education in the years ahead.

A useful way of approaching the investigation of this transition of philosophic thought from pragmatism to empiricism and back to pragmatism (and what the transitions mean for educational practice) is to focus on the role that a priori knowledge plays within these philosophic schools of thought. A priori knowledge is the knowledge we possess that is *not* based on sensory experience. Of course, much of what we know is based on our sensory experience, but there are important aspects of knowledge that are not. There are four distinct conceptions of a priori knowledge, each of which gives a different direction to the philosophic study of education and, consequently, greatly colors what we take to be the proper role of teaching. The fact that the view of a priori knowledge that we embrace can influence classroom practices makes it critically important for contemporary educators to understand these four approaches to what we know.

In a sense, the modern history of empiricism is captured in a statement in *The Case of the Philosophers' Ring*, where Lord Russell says to Mr. Holmes: "When I was very young and intelligent, I worked exclusively at mathematics.

After I grew too old for the mental effort, I turned to philosophy. And now, having exhausted my brains almost entirely, I have turned to politics."[2] This statement is a poignant summary of the development of empiricism in the twentieth century. As Larry Laudan has argued, the relativist's view of epistemological discourse is not the view that replaces empiricism but is the *end game* of empiricism.[3] The view of logical positivism, and later of logical empiricism, appears to be the opposite of that held by the "relativist fellow travelers" (as Laudan calls them), but the former is actually the source of the latter. Borrowing his conclusion, one might say that the political discourse that has become the hallmark of educational foundations is not progress over empiricism but its progeny. In an instance of pragmatist problem solving, Laudan shows that the positivists and the relativists share many assumptions.[4] (Recall that Dewey showed that the more important element in problem solving is the evaluation of common assumptions, not differences. A classical use of this method is his analysis of interest versus effort in education.)

In the nineteenth century, empiricists were concerned with the nature of mathematical knowledge because, with few exceptions, philosophers agreed that mathematics was knowledge that was not rooted in sensory experience. This presented a problem for the empiricists, who wanted to show that scientific knowledge is grounded in sensory experience. To show that mathematical knowledge was indeed knowledge and that the empiricist's view of sensory data was correct, it was necessary to develop an analytical methodology. The methodology that resulted was thought to be so potent that it could be used to deal with virtually all traditional philosophic problems.

Given that empiricism was producing many original insights into the nature of logic, mathematics, and scientific knowledge, it was only a matter of time until this methodology was put to work in the philosophic study of education. There may have been a working assumption on the part of some that the empiricist's approach to philosophy of science could be a model for philosophy of education,[5] but there was, in fact, much talk about developing "an analytic philosophy of education." I believe that those who advocated this methodology saw themselves as part of a philosophic movement that was the obvious successor to the pragmatists' approach to philosophy of education. Dewey was recognized as having made major contributions to philosophy of education, but his thinking was, nevertheless, seen as limited because of the new discoveries in philosophic methodology. In other words, Dewey was rejected, not because what he said was wrong or misguided, but because there were now better ways of "doing philosophy," an expression frequently used by empiricists.

By the last quarter of the twentieth century, it was clear that empiricism and its analytic methodology were receiving profound criticisms from several different directions. Some consider Thomas Kuhn's *Structure of Scientific Revolutions* (1962) to be the *coup de grace* for empiricism.[6] Even if Kuhn's analysis of the historical development of science had not appeared, studies in cognitive psychology and neuroscience would have eventually overthrown empiricism. Analytic philosophy sought to build its methodology on a science-free foundation, a methodology divorced from the knowledge of the physiology of knowing. Philip Kitcher seems to place the headstone when he suggests that analytic philosophy may be seen as nothing more than "an odd blip"[7] in the history of philosophy.

As serious doubts arose about the adequacy of the tenets of empiricist philosophy and its analytic methodology, especially its ability to explain scientific knowledge, many concluded that the problems philosophy posed, such as What is knowledge? could not be answered. For the relativists, philosophy of education is, at best, an edifying conversation about education that both (a) avoids the errors of taking epistemology seriously and (b) allows politics to be smuggled in as philosophy. Today, it is stating the obvious to say that the content of philosophy of education is much more political than philosophic. Consider remarks Kitcher made in 1992: "A disturbingly large number of contemporary intellectuals perceive post-Fregean, 'analytic,' 'pure' philosophy as having collapsed. They conclude that this is the death of philosophy, and that succession passes variously to history, sociology, or literary theory. By focusing on the viability of traditional naturalism, I have tried to show that there are relatively unappreciated possibilities of extending the tradition."[8]

My goal is to explore what Kitcher called the "unappreciated possibilities of extending the tradition" of philosophy of education in ways that further its critical and constructive tasks. As I have indicated, a major unappreciated possibility is the work of John Dewey, whose name and words are ubiquitous within philosophy of education literature although his work remains incomprehensible to many educators (and perhaps to some philosophers of education). He is quoted in the educational literature in much the way that some quote the Bible or extract sentences from the works of Shakespeare; that is, in place of a comprehensive and penetrating understanding of the guiding values in education, they cite statements that are, in spite of their poetic character, relatively mindless bromides that cannot free us from the charge of philosophic morbidity.

Philosophy of education has never been widely accepted by educators as a source of wisdom for what they do, and for years, philosophy of education courses have been under siege. On many campuses these courses have imploded or been absorbed by other areas of study. If confidence in philosophy in general and in philosophic analysis in particular has declined, as the remarks of Kitcher suggest, then the confidence levels for philosophy of education within the field of education will be no better. The criticism of educational theories and practices has, to a great extent, already become the office of other types of thought. Were it not for the vigorous work being done in epistemology and philosophy of science, one might conclude that this is how it should be; if philosophy of education has atrophied, then it is the province of other academic areas to perform the critical function. I believe, however, that if philosophy of education is viewed within the context of both contemporary epistemological thought and traditional pragmatism, it will be discovered that it has not atrophied and currently has the wherewithal to reassert itself. In what follows, I will attempt to show that philosophy of education can be reinvigorated as *philosophic* inquiry.

Naturalizing Philosophy of Education

During the preempiricist period in twentieth-century philosophy, much of philosophic activity could be characterized as *speculative* or *synthetic;* that is, philosophers of this epoch still saw their task as constructing coherent theories of the true, the good, and the beautiful. To provide this account, the speculative philosophers were free to draw from any area of knowledge, but as science was not as developed as it is today, they were not confronted with an endless flow of data and hypotheses about the nature of the development of our cognitive processes. As science grew, it tended to encroach on the content of speculative philosophy, making much of this content appear to be armchair science.

Empiricists, or analytic philosophers, as they called themselves, separated from speculative philosophy by taking the position that the problems that speculative or synthetic philosophy were investigating were not legitimate ones and would disappear if philosophers paid proper attention to language and meaning. In place of building great linguistic edifices, as they saw the speculative philosophers doing, the analysts saw their task as taking language apart into its most basic elements in order to establish its rules. They were clearly anticonstructive and antisynthetic, and they sought to clean up the distinction between philosophy and nonphilosophy. A famous analytic philosopher was lecturing on this point when one of his students complained that all philosophy did was disassemble theories, but it never built anything. To this the analytic philosopher replied, it was written that Hercules had to clean the Augean stables, but it was not written that he had to refill them.

The writings of the pragmatists arose within a context of, and in opposition to, speculative philosophy. Their goal was to naturalize epistemology, metaphysics, and axiology. But the empiricists viewed the pragmatists as part of the preanalytic, speculative period because they would not separate themselves from scientific commitments. As Kitcher notes, preanalytic or, "PreFregean modern philosophy was distinguished not only by its emphasis on problems of knowledge, but also by its willingness to draw on the ideas of the emerging sciences, to cull concepts from ventures in psychology and physics, later still to find inspiration in Darwin."[9] Dewey and the naturalists did draw inspiration from Darwin's evolutionary account of human existence and from the scientific methods that had led, through Einstein, to an entirely different conception of the universe. Dewey argued that this same mode of thought that revolutionized the way we understand the world and our place in it could be turned on all human problems, including psychology, morals, and even philosophy itself.

The empiricists' explicit goal was to provide a decontextualized view of knowledge. The plan was to develop a conception of a priori knowledge that could be justified prior to all sensory experience but could be used to organize that experience. This decontextualized approach to the foundations of science has received sufficient criticism for us to investigate the possibility of grounding our knowledge in a *contextualized* or pragmatic view of a priori knowledge. This point is further supported, as we shall see, by recent arguments in philosophy of science that suggest that a pragmatic view of the goals of inquiry, as well as their justification, is being taken seriously by many philosophers. As Steven Stich observes, "There is a long tradition in epistemology which would reject out of hand any proposal that makes epistemological questions dependent on empirical findings or technological developments. But that is a tradition which I, in the company of a growing number of philosophers, take to be sterile and moribund."[10] But he also says that there is an epistemological tradition "tracing to James and Dewey" that "finds nothing untoward in the suggestion that epistemology is inseparable from science and technology."[11] The question is, how do we make use of scientific results in philosophic studies?

When the promise of analytic philosophy of education was not fulfilled, many came to the conclusion that analytic philosophy had inherent limitations that could not take the field beyond what Dewey had already charted. During the period in which analytic philosophy dominated philosophy of education, there were those who advocated an ideological approach to the study of education, and as analytic philosophy was clearly running out of fresh insights into educational concepts, the emerging ideological movements found space for development. When people began to speak of the passing of the analytic movement in philosophy of education, the ideological approach was already well entrenched in the field and had some warrant for claiming that it was the rightful successor to empiricism.

I will discuss Kuhn's arguments in the following chapter, but for now, consider his major conclusion: "As in political revolutions, so in paradigm choice—there is no standard higher than the assent of the relevant community."[12] Many take this to mean that science is nothing more than politics in technical clothing. Their argument goes as follows: The assertions we call "scientific" have no greater epistemological warrant than claims made by any other group. Any political community has the right to make and believe its own assertions, and no community has the right to claim that its assertions are more adequate than the assertions of any other community. Since communities are formed by interests consciously shared, claims that advance those interests are readily believable by the members of that community. The notion that there is some objective third-party methodology that could settle conflicts among communities is considered by many to have been refuted by Kuhn's thesis. When one group cites scientific evidence to support its policies, another group views this appeal to science as a self-serving attack clothed in what a naive public takes to be objective truth. This view is not only at work in the study of education, but it is being taught as philosophy of education on many campuses.

If science is suspect, then how shall we know about personal development, teaching, and schooling? There is now a hollowing-out of the teacher education programs by education professors who believe that teachers can be prepared through a process of pooled, anecdotal stories generated by collections of assorted personal histories. By reading and sharing such stories, education students are said to be preparing to teach. Any notion of competence is eschewed, and students are graduated having been led to believe that there are no theories of learning or teaching. This line of reasoning makes fundamental epistemological mistakes. Simply because there is an epistemological difficulty with the empiricists' methodology of language analysis, we are not thereby freed from all epistemological requirements. On what basis do we claim that our past experience is a guide to the future? On what grounds do we claim that someone's experience will be of value to another person?

One great achievement of empiricism is the thorough evaluation of theories of inductive inference, especially those based on principles such as the uniformity of nature. The reason that we know the sun will rise tomorrow goes profoundly beyond the fact that it always has. Shared experience, common experiences, and repeated experiences are of little value without some epistemology to give form and direction to subsequent experience. The fact that a hundred teachers report that they have solved the same problem in the same way is not the convergence of evidence unless we know that this was a random sequence of independent events.[13] Many contemporary epistemologists do not take a skeptical view of science and instead claim that if we reconnect our thinking with the epistemologists of the preanalytic period, we will discover that the science-is-politics proposition is ill-conceived. It is the thesis of this book that philosophy of education must hold itself to the same standards as philosophy of science and epistemology.

I want to show that philosophy of education in the postanalytic period (what some might call the postempiricist period) must place even greater epistemological demands on itself than it did during the analytic period. To warrant this line of thinking, I will, as the title suggests, look to Dewey's epistemological ideas. To set out to reconnect the postanalytic with the preanalytic period in philosophy of education inevitably leads to John Dewey, whose writings tell us about the seminal role of scientific thinking in the history of philosophy and human existence. Moreover, I believe that Dewey cannot be appreciated without attention to the arguments and issues we find in contemporary philosophy of science.

Those not well versed in epistemology might conclude that the field of philosophy of education has evolved since midcentury through three philosophic eras: pragmatism, analytic philosophy, and the ideological present. To understand why this view is incorrect, we must consider certain central epistemological issues. Those who are knowledgeable about the philosophic past have the wherewithal to reconnect with it, draw sustenance from it, and give direction to education in the postanalytic period. Unfortunately, the skepticism about speculative philosophy among philosophers of education of the analytic period led them to ignore or depreciate the value of preanalytic philosophy. History has not been kind to movements that sought to reject completely what came before and to begin anew, freed of all past contaminations. It is an old pragmatist precept that those who do not respect the continuity of thought find little to reconstruct when the serious problems appear, as they always do.

Can Conceptual Analysis Be Naturalized?

In addition to using the notion of a priori knowledge as a way of explaining the changes occurring in philosophy and philosophy of education, I want to focus on the methodology of conceptual analysis. This secondary focus assumes that the methodology of conceptual analysis has been, and will continue to be, an important tool for identifying and evaluating the philosophic dimensions of educational thought and conduct. In other words, I am not willing to grant that the methodology of conceptual analysis is so inextricably tied to empiricism that it falls with empiricism. I claim that progress in philosophy of education requires improvement in our understanding of this methodology. By focusing on the nature of a priori knowledge, we have a way to examine and evaluate the methodology of conceptual analysis and to explore the ways it can be improved. We must understand why empiricism and its view of conceptual analysis is being rejected because an understanding of the basis of this rejection provides a new sense of direction for analytical thought.

The analytic philosophers of education were critical of Dewey, not because he could be read as doing language analysis, but because he did so in a "programmatic" way. That is, when Dewey "reconstructed" the meaning of a term such as *education* (which is still the locus classicus), the empiricists claimed that he introduced his values into the discourse in a sub rosa fashion. The language analysts wanted to be true to language and rationality, and some of them said that Dewey was using a different standard for the enucleation of the meaning of terms. When Dewey is judged from the perspective of the analytic period, his work, not surprisingly, is seen as inadequate. But if the analytic perspective is suspect, then the judgment against Dewey's approach to meaning deserves a new trial.

The value of having an adequate methodology of conceptual analysis is as important today as it ever was. Philosophy of education in the years ahead will be giving considerable attention to the claims emerging from cognitive science about the nature of intelligence and how it is nurtured. Sorting out the arguments of the computationalists, neural network theorists, and the folk psychologists requires conceptual analysis. Consider John Searle's recent study, in which he questioned what he claims is a common assumption of cognitive scientists, "that the question of whether brain processes are computational is just a plain empirical question . . . to be settled by factual investigation in the same way that such questions as whether the heart is a pump or whether green leaves do photosynthesis were settled as matters of fact."[14] Many cognitive scientists, according to Searle, see nothing philosophic in this matter. But as Searle further notes, "we are in a peculiar situation where there is little theoretical agreement among the practitioners on such absolutely fundamental questions as, What exactly is a digital computer? What exactly is a symbol? What exactly is an algorithm? What exactly is a computational process? Under what physical conditions exactly are two systems implementing the same program?"[15] These questions obviously require the services of an adequate methodology of conceptual analysis as much as any questions asked in philosophy since the time of Aristotle. The fact that empiricism's version of how to do conceptual analysis has lost its luster is not a reason to think that conceptual analysis is any less an important tool for the investigation of present philosophic concerns. The problem is to characterize its methodology and to provide a justification thereof.

As the questions asked by Searle indicate, the methodology of conceptual analysis required to deal with the philosophic problems being posed today must be able to integrate the findings from science and philosophy. When asked within cognitive science, Searle's question "What exactly is a computational process?" involves elements of logic, mathematics, philosophy of mathematics, epistemology, artificial intelligence, cognitive psychology, and so forth. To delimit arbitrarily the traditional literatures that are or are not relevant to this question is an indefensible strategy. Conceptual analysis must be able to look into any area that seems promising.

The Challenge to Normative Inquiry:
Instrumentalism or Utopianism?

Empiricism was never able to give a very satisfying account of moral knowledge, and when many in philosophy of education felt that it could not give an account of scientific knowledge either, there was a general turning away from moral and epistemological inquiry and a move toward ideological activity. Kuhn's thesis seemed to support a community relativism, and some concluded that it is the business of educational foundations to set out to build utopian communities.[16] If successful normative inquiry is impossible, then ideological consistency might be all that one could hope for. Let's make sure that we understand what this conclusion means.

Christine Korsgaard presents the matter as follows:

> A lower animal's attention is focused on the world. Its perceptions are its beliefs and its desires are its will. It is engaged in conscious activities, but it is not conscious *of* them. That is, they are not the objects if its attention. But we humans turn our attention on to our perceptions and desires themselves, on to our own mental activities, and we are conscious *of* them. That is why we can think *about* them. . . . And this sets us a problem no other animal has. It is the problem of the normative. For our capacity to focus our attention on to our own mental activities is also a capacity to distance ourselves from them, and to call them into question. . . . Scepticism about the good and the right is not scepticism about the existence of intrinsically normative entities. It is the view that the problems that reflection sets for us are insolvable, that the questions to which it gives rise have no answers.[17]

If we distance ourselves from our beliefs and arguments about education, call them into question, and evaluate them, we will find a great drama playing out before us. As the relativism constitutive of empiricism's swan song grows louder, can the naturalists save normative studies, or will might make right after all?

If pragmatism is to be reinvigorated within philosophy of education, then it must (a) offer a viable account of normative inquiry and (b) show why utopian thinking is misguided and even undemocratic. As I said before, how we view the nature of a priori knowledge is the major distinguishing feature between the four views of knowledge to be discussed in the following chapters, but it is also possible to use this analysis of a priori knowledge to show the inadequacy of much of contemporary philosophy of education.

It is the thesis of this book that philosophy of education must hold itself to the same standards as philosophy of science and epistemology. Today, philosophy of education has moved away from the regime of epistemology in search of what is frequently referred to as postmodernism. Perhaps the first intellectual struggle of the twenty-first century will be over the following question: Which view shall we embrace, political ideology or naturalism? The political ideologues want us to believe that ideology is the proper replacement for empiricism and that empiricism's inadequacies are sufficient reason to replace epistemological discourse with political discourse. But the return to naturalized epistemology in philosophy presents an alternative to this view. With the reassertion of pragmatism in epistemology and philosophy of science, it is long past time for its reemergence in philosophy of education.

Let us admit the case of the ideologues. It is our problem, not theirs, to show that defensible normative inquiry is possible. It is our problem, not theirs, to present a methodology of conceptual analysis that can replace that of the analytic period. These problems have great import. Teaching and schooling are the resources of the information age; if we are unable to provide a warrant for normative studies, then those who reject the continuity of human intelligence and embrace a narrow (often authoritarian) view of thought and speech will define the field. I, of course, believe that we can reestablish the normative warrant for philosophy of education by investigating the epistemology being pursued in philosophy of science and that by using these studies to reframe the problems that characterize the philosophy of education, we will be, as Stanley Cavell says, "leaping free of enforced speech, so succeeding it. Thus is philosophy successful."[18]

2

THE EMPIRICISTIC CONCEPTION
OF A PRIORI KNOWLEDGE

Introduction

UNDERSTANDING THE VARIOUS conceptions of a priori knowledge (what we know that is not based on sensory experience) gives us a well-lighted avenue to understanding what makes different philosophies different. We begin with the empiricists' view of a priori knowledge, because it is the most common in educational research and in recent philosophy of education.

From the time of Aristotle, philosophers have seen themselves as guardians of the concept of rationality and, through the ages, have attempted to improve our understanding of it. More than a hundred years ago, Gottlob Frege received much acclaim for his analysis of the methodology of mathematics—an analysis thought to be so powerful that many philosophers came to believe that the road to improving our conception of rationality had been found.[1]

Frege's analysis of mathematics became, according to Kitcher, an "emblem" for the new view of philosophic methodology.

> Frege's investigations are commonly viewed as a decisive turn, one that de-throned epistemology from its central position among the philosophical disciplines and that set the philosophy of language in its place. In retrospect, we can trace a great lineage from Frege, leading through Russell, Wittgenstein, and Rudolf Carnap to the professional philosophy practiced in Britain, North America, Australasia and Scandinavia in the postwar years. Distinguished by its emphasis on logical analysis, the analytic movement, the "linguistic turn," differs from earlier philosophical endeavors in its method as well as in its ordering of philosophical problems. For at least a period, philosophers could be confident of their professional standing, priding themselves on the presence of a method—the method of conceptual analysis—which they, and they alone, were trained to use.[2]

The view that emerged from these efforts is referred to as First Philosophy, because the questions properly addressed by philosophy are always answered *prior* to those studied in the sciences. "Frege's opposition to what he perceived as intrusions from psychology to biology is evident from celebrated passages in the *Grundlagen*. The methodological stance he inspired becomes explicit in propositions of the *Tractatus*."[3] Ludwig Wittgenstein, in the *Tractatus*, holds that philosophy is not one of the natural sciences (*Die Philosophie ist keine der Naturwissenschaften*);[4] moreover, psychology is no more relevant to philosophy than any other science (*Die Psychologie ist der Philosophie nicht verwandter als irgendeine andere Naturwissenschaft*).[5] Clearly, philosophic analysis must be conducted prior to any consideration of scientific results or any other claims about the actual world in which we find ourselves.

The major challenge to the logical empiricists' goal of presenting a rational account of scientific thinking is David Hume, whose argument was as follows: all justification must be deductive or inductive; so a justification of inductive inference must be deductive or inductive. Deductive arguments are truth preserving in that if the premises are true and the rules of deductive inference are followed, then the conclusion must be true. Inductive arguments are ampliative in that their conclusions always possess greater content than their premises. Deductive arguments do not generate any additional truths; they only preserve it, while inductive arguments amplify what is known. Obviously, scientific inquiry during the last two hundred years has been epistemologically ampliative. The problem is, how?

Hume holds that deduction is not at all useful in justifying inductive inference because to justify scientific inference deductively we would have to make scientific methodology the conclusion of a deductive argument whose premises are known to be true. If the premises are analytically true, then they can tell us nothing about this universe, including justified scientific inferences. If the premises are synthetically true, then we have justified scientific inference in terms of certain premises. How do we know these premises are true? If they are justified deductively, then they are the conclusions of yet other deductive arguments. But then we wonder how we know that the premises of this second deductive argument are true. Perhaps we could develop a third deductive argument in which the premises of the second argument are the conclusion of the third argument. But this is going to regress forever—thus Hume's conclusion that a deductive strategy for the justification of inductive inference is going to lead to an infinite regress.

Perhaps we could justify inductive inferences inductively. This would require making the methodology of inductive inferences the conclusion of an inductive argument. As Hume argued, this approach seeks to use the methodology in question to justify itself. On the face of it, this is a circular argument. Scientific inferences must be either deductive or inductive inferences, and this means that they lead either to an infinite regress or to circular reasoning. Much of the work in empiricism since World War II has been devoted to the problem of constructing an account of scientific knowledge based on an adequate theory of inductive inference.

If Hume is correct, we do not have the scientific knowledge we think we do; if scientific inferences are actually producing irrational beliefs, then what about our moral beliefs? If scientific knowledge is suspect, then how could one have moral knowledge? How could we justify this curriculum over that one? How could we know which teaching methods are most effective? Hume's skepticism resonates through all of human knowledge.

In Hume's time, before the knowledge explosion brought on by the growth in scientific research of the nineteenth and twentieth centuries, one could wonder about the potential limits of human understanding. In our time, the question has changed to that of *explaining* the nature of the extraordinary growth in scientific research. But the spirit of Hume's problem is still with us. So while we are less inclined to view human knowledge as having the restrictive limits that Hume's epistemology requires, we nevertheless must wonder if what we take to be great achievements in human objectivity and understanding are not in reality great fictitious accounts built on self-indulgent relativism. Have we captured in our methods the key to understanding nature, or have we built a great ideological system—one that we have all bought into, cognitively? Is the scientific approach to fixing belief any better than any other method, or is it just another mythical phenomenon of a particular time? In short, is the scientific approach to understanding our environment any more rational that any other way of fixing belief?

The Analytic Conception of the A Priori

Philosophers working in the Frege-Russell-Wittgenstein-Carnap tradition sought to develop an account of the rationality of scientific methodology by characterizing scientific inference and explanation in terms of what can be known with certainty. The great cognitive achievements of science in the eighteenth and nineteenth centuries must be the result of thought that has built a foundation more firm than anything yet described by philosophers. Of all of the statements thought and experience can generate, two types can be asserted with great confidence: analytic statements (logical truths) and direct observation statements (reports of sensory data). Upon these two certitudes, and the rules of deductive inference, empiricism attempted to build an adequate account of scientific rationality.

Analytic Statements

A statement is analytic if and only if its truth can be established solely by the rules of language. Such statements can be created in two ways: (1) stipulative definition and (2) tautology. A stipulative definition establishes an arbitrary rule for using a word in a certain way. It may be stipulated that 'sloop' refers to a sailboat with one mast, two sails, and a single jib. In actual linguistic practice 'sloop' may be used in other ways, but the stipulative definition lays down a rule that will be used in a given context of research. If other researchers come to accept this stipulation, then it may become the standard definition in a given research field.

Stipulative definitions are often used in sets in social science to form what is referred to as a "typology"—an arbitrary set of stated stipulations that comprise a category system for organizing data, with the only requirement being that the typology contain categories that are mutually exclusive and jointly exhaustive.

A tautology is a statement whose denial produces a contradiction. It is sometimes described as a statement that cannot both be understood and denied. A contradiction would be produced if we were to claim that the statement 'Either A or not A' is false. But why are contradictions so abhorrent to logicians? Contradictions are statements from which any arbitrary statement may be demonstrated. Consider the following deductive argument.

1. A and not A (by hypothesis, a contradiction)
2. A (simplification: conjuncts may be separated)
3. Not A (simplification: conjuncts may be separated)[6]
4. A or B (addition of an arbitrary statement to 2)
5. Not A implies B (transportation of 4)
6. B (5, 3, modus ponens)[7]

In step four, an arbitrary statement, B, is disjoined with a true statement. For example, if we know that '2 + 2 = 4' is a true statement, then 'Either (2 + 2 = 4) or (2 + 2 = 5)' is true. Disjunctive statements (*or*-statements) require only that one of the disjuncts be true for the statement to be true. This means that any statement can be disjoined with a statement known to be true, with the result being a true statement. The arbitrary statement B, in the above argument, has been deduced from the premises. This means that any theory that contains a contradiction has every proposition as its logical consequence. An inconsistent theory entails every statement.

But how does the denial of a tautology produce a contradiction? Consider the following tautological statement: A or not A. We make it the first premise in the following deduction.

1. A or not A (tautology)
2. Not (A or not A) (negation of 1, per hypothesis)
3. (Not A) and not (not A) (De Morgan's theorem on 2)
4. Not A and A (double negation on 3)

The statement in step four is a contradiction. The above argument shows that the denial of the tautology in step one leads to a contradiction (which means, as we have just seen, that any statement can be deduced from it). This is what is meant when it is said that tautologies cannot be consistently denied. So tautologies are statements that we know for sure are true in all possible worlds, come what may in actual experience. (Actually a better way to make this point is to say that tautologies are true no matter what this universe turns out to be.) To gain this special status among the set of all possible statements, analytic statements have to devoid themselves of empirical content. By giving up all empirical content, these statements (according to empiricists) are able to organize the plethora of data statements generated by scientific work. This was Gilbert Ryle's point: "It is . . . no freak of history that Wittgenstein, in his *Tractatus*, was concerned, perhaps above all else, to show how the propositions of Formal Logic and, derivatively, those of philosophy are condemned to be uninformative about the world and yet able, in some important way, to be clarificatory of those propositions that are informative about the world, reporting no matters of fact yet correcting our mishandlings of reported matters of fact."[8] Formal logic maintains consistency within our claims about the universe by providing a framework within which to organize our experiencing of the universe.

Synthetic Statements

To have information about the universe requires more than empty analytic statements. If we are to have knowledge of this universe, we have to have a different type of statement—one whose truth is established by reference to this universe. Through the senses we gain information about the universe. 'This A is a B' (where 'A' and 'B' are observation terms) is as basic a factual claim as one can think of. By means of direct inspection, it is possible to obtain specific facts about the universe. Through many such observations, data are generated that can support general conclusions. Empiricists have always shown some concern for the adequacy of this sensory link between person and universe. Consider, for example, the traditional token mentioning of the twig sticking out of the water that appears bent but is not.

Logic provides the framework that organizes all the specific observation reports generated by experiments and collected by observers in the field and thereby provides the structure for scientific knowledge. This approach is taken to be justified because it assumes nothing about the nature of the world or universe in advance of actual observation. In this sense, empiricistic methodology is tabula rasa or blank slate methodology. The logical truths are devoid of content and, hence, acceptable; and since the observation statements are replicatible and possess high inter-rater reliability, they are objective. Empiricists take this to be a firm foundation for science.

Before examining alternatives to this approach, we should consider a fresh way to think of the difference between sentences thought to be true because of sensory data or observation and sentences thought to be true because of logical relationship. As Raymond Kurzweil has noted:

> Two types of thought processes coexist in our brains. . . . Perhaps most cited as a uniquely human form of intelligence is the *logical* process involved in solving problems and playing games. A more ubiquitous form of intelligence that we share with most of the earth's higher animal species is the ability to *recognize patterns* from our visual, auditory, and tactile senses. We appear to have substantial control over the sequential steps required for logical thought. In contrast, pattern recognition, while very complex and involving several levels of abstraction, seems to happen without our conscious direction.[9]

Kurzweil further observes that the field of artificial intelligence has had great success in emulating logical thinking but much less with emulating animal abilities. The main problem has been "the subtleties of vision, our most powerful sense."[10]

Consider the distinction between *gradual versus catastrophic thinking:* "The ability of the human brain to process visual images typically degrades the same way that a holographic (three-dimensional, laser-generated) picture degrades. Failure of individual elements subtract only marginally from the overall result. Logical processes are quite different. Failure of any step in a chain of logical deductions and inferences dooms the rest of the thought process."[11] Any mistake in deductive logic will produce an invalid conclusion, so we must be very careful about the formal aspects of scientific knowledge. Computers can readily perform the deductive logical thinking more quickly and more accurately than can we, and since errors are both catastrophic and more typical of people than machines, it makes sense to think of computers as "power tools for the mind."[12] In the area of sensory or perceptual knowledge, however, any one mistake typically does not matter very much. In a set of observations, one might find a few statements that are incorrect. The old objection to using observation in reason was that the senses can play tricks on us. Kurzweil's point is that the existence of incorrect datum statements is not very damaging to research.

What is important in visual perception is the detection of edges. "Changes involving tiny regions can probably be considered to be non-information-bearing visual noise. . . . we are primarily interested in sudden and consistent alterations in color or shading from one region to another."[13] This point is reinforcing to tabula rasa theorists in that it supports their placing so much emphasis on, and trust in, sensory data.

A Priori Versus A Posteriori Knowledge

Finally, we should distinguish between a priori and a posteriori knowledge. A priori knowledge is not derived from experience and so may be embraced regardless of actual experience. A posteriori knowledge is knowledge derived directly from experience. An analytic statement is true because of logic and stipulative definition, and it is contrasted with synthetic statements that are true or false on actual observational evidence. The expression 'analytic a priori' is going to be seen as redundant by empiricists because analytic statements are the only form of a priori knowledge, that is, statements whose truth can be established by reference to the rules of language.

Philosophy of Education as First Philosophy

With such a philosophically prominent method at hand, it was only to be expected that it would be put to work in philosophy of education, an emerging field in need of a methodology that would increase its confidence, pride, and professional standing. The problems to be investigated by First Philosophy of education are the questions for which we must have answers before other questions can be pursued—the so-called prior questions of analytic philosophy. As

Jonas Soltis states in his respected book on the methods of conceptual analysis in education, "They are questions of meaning, and, as such, generally are nonsubstantive; that is, they do not deal with the factual or valuational substance of the topic. Rather, they are questions that seek conceptual clarity before commitment to the substantive exploration of a topic."[14] Again it is clear that the language analysts take the meaning of words to exist prior to and apart from the uses made of them. To analyze either the facts or the values involved in teaching, for example, requires, according to the language analysts, the establishment of the prior meaning of 'teaching'. The meaning of 'teaching' is, on this view, not a consequent of what teachers do, but an antecedent.

If, as Aristotle argued, rationality is the defining characteristic of humans, then for children to be set on the path to the rational life their teachers would be required to adhere to and pursue rational standards. Israel Scheffler's book *Reason and Teaching* contains a 1953 essay entitled "Toward an Analytic Philosophy of Education."[15] Not all work that was thought to be forwarding analytic philosophy of education was imported from the literature of general philosophy, but much of Scheffler's educational writings are obvious applications of conclusions from the philosophic literature to education.

The question of knowing is an important example. The traditional answer given by analytic philosophy is known in philosophy as the *justified true belief* view. Scheffler, however, considered what this analysis of knowledge meant for teaching.[16] The belief condition requires the conviction of the knower, and Scheffler considered learning the process that led to belief. He holds that to say a person believes something is to say that he or she has learned it but not that he or she knows it. "To say that someone has learned that Q, does not so commit us [to the truth of Q]; we are, in general, limited only to the claim that he has come to believe that Q."[17] For Scheffler, learning is the process that produces belief and is preepistemological in the sense that learning is the process that achieves one of the conditions of knowing but is not itself one of those conditions.

Teaching should not only produce learning but it should do so under the limited conditions of rationality or rational inquiry. "The person engaged in teaching does not merely want to bring about belief, but to bring it about through the exercise of free rational judgment by the student. This is what distinguishes teaching from propaganda or debating. . . . Teaching, it might be said, involves trying to bring about learning under the severe restrictions of *manner*—that is to say, within the limitations imposed by the framework of rational discussion" (emphasis in original).[18] Scheffler's point is that belief is fixed as a result of learning, which teaching can bring about; but teaching should be conducted in a rational manner, which means that it must take into account the justification condition of knowing.

Note again that the standard thesis about the concept of knowing, as well as Scheffler's application of it to educational thought, makes no reference to psychological theory or data. The disagreements over the nature of the learning process by different psychological orientations is not seen as relevant to the pursuit of conceptual questions about knowing, believing, learning, and teaching. Twenty years ago, I tried to argue that the analysts were seriously misleading philosophy of education. I said that it was "malpractice" to cut philosophizing off from what we know about the world because "A view of desirable education should be developed in light of the empirical possibility for human growth and the potential for purposeful intervention within."[19] At that time the battle seemed to be over the adequacy of thinking of philosophy of education as only a "second-order" activity.

Difficulties with First Philosophy

Why did First Philosophy fall from intellectual grace? Before I deal with this question, a caution should be raised about engaging in generational chauvinism. Empiricism was driven by some of the best philosophic thinkers of this century; its efforts in understanding scientific knowledge are legendary, and its failures provide significant insights for contemporary thought.

First Philosophy came under criticism from various points of view, but two are important for us. If any philosophy is to have credibility it has to provide answers to two related normative questions: What is knowledge? What is science? Unfortunately, First Philosophy has been shown to be unable to answer either question adequately—a situation that has led to the "death of philosophy" talk mentioned by Kitcher and Stich's comment about the "sterile and moribund" nature of philosophy that rejects "out of hand any proposal that makes epistemological questions dependent on empirical findings or technological developments."[20]

The Standard Definition of 'Knowing'

To see where the flaw appeared in the standard definition of 'knowing', let's briefly review Edmond Gettier's now famous first example.[21] Smith and Jones have both applied for the same job. Perhaps they share a hotel room, and Smith sees Jones take ten coins from the desk where Smith had placed his wallet and the ten coins the night before and put them in his pocket. Smith has been told by the president of the company, perhaps at dinner the night before, that Jones will get the job. Consider sentence (A) below.

(A) Jones is the man who will get the job, and Jones has ten coins in his pocket.

Statement (A) entails statement (B) as follows:

(B) The man who will get the job has ten coins in his pocket.

Smith sees (B) as a logical consequence of (A) and accepts (B) because of this entailment and because he has strong evidence for (A). Smith is justified in believing that (B) is true.

But in the meantime the president has decided to give the job to Smith instead of Jones. Also, by chance, it turns out that Smith has exactly ten coins in his pocket. Now (B) is true but (A) from which Smith inferred (B) is now clearly false. In his original paper Gettier states the following:

> (i) (B) is true, (ii) Smith believes that (B) is true, and (iii) Smith is justified in believing that (B) is true. But it is equally clear that Smith does not *know* that (B) is true; for (B) is true in virtue of the number of coins in Smith's pocket, while Smith does not know how many coins are in Smith's pocket, and bases his belief in (B) on a count of the coins in Jones' pocket, whom he falsely believes to be the man who will get the job.[22]

Gettier concludes that the justified, true, belief definition of 'knowing' "does not state *sufficient* conditions for someone's knowing a given proposition."[23] What are now known as "the Gettier counterexamples" stimulated much serious reflection on the adequacy of the standard definition.[24] (Steven Stich says that replying to Gettier's counterexamples has become "a thriving cottage industry.")[25]

By the late 1960s and early 1970s, many epistemologists had concluded that any analysis of knowledge must consider, as Kitcher put it, the "causal processes that generate and sustain belief on those occasions where the subject knows."[26] Having justified true belief is not enough to know. The Gettier counterexamples show that how we come to believe is an important part of knowing. If the causal processes by which we come to have beliefs is an essential element in the meaning of 'knowing', then philosophers can no longer claim that psychology has no place in the study of knowing. The reconnection of contemporary analyses of 'knowing' to preanalytic philosophy has taken place for many writers.[27] As Kitcher asks, "How could our psychological and biological capacities and limitations *fail* to be relevant to the study of human knowledge? How could our scientific understanding of ourselves—or our reflections on the history of the sciences—support the notion that answers to skepticism and organons of methodology (or, indeed, anything very much) be generated *a priori?*"[28] The shortcomings of the standard thesis about the defining conditions of 'knowing' indicate to some that First Philosophy's methodology of conceptual analysis must be reconsidered.

Methodological Foundationism

Methodological foundationism[29] is the use of the methods of First Philosophy in philosophy of science. The goal of methodological foundationism was to provide a rational account of scientific knowledge; this goal was motivated by Hume's skeptical view of the possibility of achieving scientific knowledge. To put it succinctly: methodological foundationism set out to answer Hume.

The astonishing successes of science during the last three hundred years were obviously related to the use of mathematics. For empiricists to realize their goal of providing a rational methodological foundation for the conduct and content of science, it is necessary to show that the role played by mathematics in science is the same role as analyticity within empiricist philosophy of knowledge. The obvious conclusion is that mathematics can be reduced to analytic statements and deductive inference—known in philosophy as the logicist thesis.

A hint of a difficulty within logical empiricism appeared when Alfred North Whitehead and Bertrand Russell were unable to fulfill the logicists' program of reducing mathematics to logic.[30] As it turned out, they were unable to make this reduction without making certain arbitrary choices. A set of premises or axioms could be stated from which all mathematical truths could be deduced. The difficulty is that there is more than one set of such axioms that will allow for the deduction of the mathematical truths. In other words, mathematics could not be reduced to logic in a unique fashion, and there is no way to show that one set of premises is better than another.

Why is this conclusion so devastating to empiricism? If mathematics cannot be reduced to a unique set of axioms, then it is equally reasonable to conclude that the analytic foundations of science are not unique. The goal of providing a solid foundation for science turned to dust, for the methodological foundations of science are relative and arbitrary. When the logicists' program to achieve a unique reduction of mathematics to logic seemed lost, many began to wonder as follows: if mathematics could not be translated into analytic statements (statements true solely by the rules of language), then perhaps we should have some reservation about the claims that scientific methodology could be characterized and justified by appeal only to analytic propositions and directly verifiable data statements. This is a horrible conclusion because it suggests that epistemological skepticism is not refuted by the presence of great scientific achievements.

W. V. O. Quine's Attack on the Concept of Analyticity

The conception of the analytic a priori is based on the separation of general analytic statements and observation statements. If a statement is analytic, then this does not mean that it will be analytically true in some other language. The truth of the statement is established by the rules of language. Changing languages changes the set of rules by which analyticity would be established.

Quine tries to understand the meaning of the claim that a given statement is analytic in a given language. His analysis of the idea of analyticity leads him to consider the concept of semantic rules of language, which he finds no clearer. His conclusion is that

> one is tempted to suppose in general that the truth of a statement is somehow analyzable into a linguistic component and a factual component. Given this supposition, it next seems reasonable that in some statements the factual component should be null; and these are the analytic statements. But, for all its *a priori* reasonableness, a boundary between analytic and synthetic statements simply has not been drawn. That there is such a distinction to be drawn at all is an unempirical dogma of empiricists, a metaphysical article of faith.[31]

We might say that Quine really knows how to hurt empiricists—attribute metaphysical faith and dogmatic thinking to them, attributes empiricists abhor.

Quine holds that any methodology for achieving knowledge is going to be, as Kitcher put it, "dependent on our absorption of ancestral lore, so that we are always implicitly dependent on the struggles of our predecessors to fashion a language apt for the description of the world."[32] Just as Whitehead and Russell were unable to reduce mathematics to logic, Quine holds that we cannot reconstruct our cognitive history in terms of a refined set of analytic principles.

Is Theory-Free Observation Possible?

While Quine's attacks on analyticity were treated with deference by logical empiricists, they never seemed especially threatened by them. This was not the case for Kuhn's attack on the notion of a theory-independent observation language. Some claim that it was Kuhn's book, *The Structure of Scientific Revolutions,* that brought down First Philosophy in philosophy of science and that because of this it is the most important book in philosophy of the twentieth century.[33] In general terms, Kuhn showed that the history of science revealed conclusions about the nature of scientific methodology that did not accord with those being advanced within First Philosophy. Kuhn asked the naturalists' question, "How could the history of science fail to be a source of phenomena to which theories about knowledge may legitimately be asked to apply?"[34] This is the challenge to First Philosophy. How could it be that theories of biological capacity, psychological processes, and the historical development of scientific knowledge are not relevant to the work of epistemologists?

For a time it was believed that the distinction between logic-in-use and a reconstructed logic-for-science protected the First Philosophy analyses from the "factual" arguments of the historians and sociologists of science, but it turned out that Kuhn's framework for investigating science was more comprehensive than the methodology used by the analysts. Moreover, Kuhn's account appeared at a time when there were serious doubts about analytical philosophy's ability to provide an answer to the problem of rational theory choice or what some call the problem of developing a rational account of inductive inference.[35]

Kuhn's naturalistic studies of science became popular in part because of his appeal to "paradigms" and "paradigm shifts," notions that found favor with many—even with those who had no idea of what he meant. Paradigms are in a sense models, and in the education literature there has always been an interest in models of teaching. But what is epistemically important about paradigms is the *standards* they establish. A paradigm is a kind of methodological regime that gives commonality to diverse and sometimes chaotic scientific activity.[36]

The more philosophically interesting criticism of Kuhn's view is that a paradigm shift is, in the end, a sociopolitical process: "As in political revolutions, so in paradigm choice—there is no standard higher than the assent of the relevant community."[37] Some took this view to mean that the norms for doing science are arbitrary; it is no wonder that the logical empiricists, committed to the development of a conception of scientific rationality, fought hard against Kuhn's thesis.[38] Nevertheless, the history of science and its evidence could not be denied.

A study suggested by Nelson Goodman presents more trouble for empiricism. Subjects were placed before a computer monitor on which only a single dot could be seen. As the subjects watched the screen, the first dot was erased and a second dot in a second color appeared. The positions of the dots and the colors used were randomly selected. (I like to think of the first dot as blue and the second dot as green. Recall that it was in Goodman's *Fact, Fiction, and Forecast* that the "grue/bleen" problem was first presented. The "new riddle of induction" concerned something that was blue up to time *t*, then green after *t*; things that possessed this property are bleen.)[39]

The subjects observe a blue dot on a dark computer monitor. In a nanosecond that blue dot disappears and a green dot appears some distance from the original blue dot. Children could program a computer to do this. What is troubling for empiricists is the fact that all subjects reported that the blue dot began to move and ended up green in its new position. Moreover, subjects point to the place on the screen *where the dot changed* color. We know that the dot did not move and did not change color, but this is not the point. Subjects report that the dot changed to green before it came to a stop in its new location. The evidence of the second dot's color and location came together, yet subjects report that they saw the dot change color before it got to its new location. Obviously their brains were interpreting the evidence and arriving at a false thesis about what happened. The form or structure of the brain is involved in perception of the universe. Goodman's study shows that the sensory data notion is misleading and should be rejected by epistemologists. (Daniel Dennett's theory developed in *Consciousness Explained* makes use of this sort of evidence.)[40]

As the discussions of the role of observations and paradigms in scientific inquiry developed, it came to be accepted, as Patricia Churchland put it, that "Bare facts, neutral observation, theory-independent access to the world, and absolute foundations have gone to the wall with logical empiricism."[41] Some paradigm or conceptual framework is required to do science. This framework serves to underwrite observations made as part of the data collection process.

One could think of Kuhn's view in Piagetian terms, though, of course, Kuhn is not a Kantian; we use our schemas to assimilate (in the Kantian sense of observation) the universe. The schemas are so familiar that we do not even remember that they are there. At some point, however, assimilation no longer seems to be working. At first we make every effort to force the schemas to work for us, but eventually we change our schemas so that better assimilations are possible. Piaget refers to these changes as accommodations, which are ontogenetic changes, whereas Kuhn refers to them as scientific revolutions, which are phylogenetic changes. Synthetic a priori concepts are relevant to ontogenetic changes, but they make no sense for phylogenetic ones.

As R. N. Giere sees it, a major obstacle to our understanding science is that we "do not seriously consider the possibility that rationality might not be an especially useful concept for understanding modern science."[42] He thinks that in their efforts to be true to their disciplinary traditions and methodology, philosophers of science have failed their subject matter—science. This thought should, I think, give us pause. If the history of the analytical period reveals that we have not come to an adequate understanding of science because of making rationality the central organizing concept, then one wonders about the study of teaching; is it possible that the analytical methodology developed around the concept of rationality has failed our subject matter?

Another point is important. Logical empiricism sought to provide a "rational reconstruction" of scientific methodology and knowledge by creating an epistemological foundation built of logic and mathematics. Dewey and the naturalists objected that scientific thought was being shoehorned into an a priori logical structure. Kuhn's historical analysis of the development of scientific knowledge came to the same conclusion. What have we learned from the analytic era of philosophic thought? Consider Searle's statement about the current thinking in cognitive science.

> In short, the sense of information processing that is used in cognitive science is *at much too high a level of abstraction to capture the concrete biological reality of intrinsic intentionality.* The "information" in the brain is always specific to some modality or the other. It is specific to thought, or vision, or hearing, or touch, for example. The level of information processing described in the cognitive science computational models of cognition, on the other hand, is simply a matter of getting a set of symbols as output in response to a set of symbols as input. . . . To confuse these [concrete biological] events and processes with formal symbol manipulation is *to confuse the reality with the model.* [Emphasis added][43]

The shoehorning for which logical empiricism was criticized reappears in cognitive science. In its urge to bring together the various areas of cognitive inquiry, cognitive science is now in danger of repeating previous mistakes.[44]

Contemporary Methodological Foundationism

There are two contemporary versions of methodological foundationism that, while criticized, represent the most viable accounts of scientific inference available within empiricism.

Karl Popper's Falsifiability Theory

Popper's approach was to replace, in Imre Lakatos's words, "the central problem of classical rationality, *the old problem of foundations*, with *the new problem of fallible-critical growth*, and started to elaborate objective standards of the growth" (emphasis in original).[45] And how did Popper perform this replacement? He used the logical principle of modus tollens to argue that the scientific method of inference is a matter of forming a conjecture (which derived from the psychological context of discovery), and then testing this conjecture by confronting it with the consequences to which it was committed. Consider first the argument form known as modus tollens.

> If this thing is a horse, then it is an animal.
> This thing is not an animal.

> Therefore, this thing is not a horse.

In general:

> If this x is an A, then it is also a B.
> This x is not a B.

> Therefore, this x is not an A.

The first sentence in the argument has two parts: "If this x is an A" is the antecedent and "then, it is a B" is the consequent. The second sentence in the argument denies the consequent; it claims that the part of the first sentence after the comma is false. The conclusion of the argument denies the antecedent. Modus tollens is an argument that denies the antecedent by denying the consequent.

So how does this tell us anything about science? We can use the modus tollens form to conceptualize a scientific inference.

If theory T is true, then observation O will occur.
O did not occur.

Therefore, theory T is not true.

The first sentence implies that given a theory, one can deduce observable consequences from it. Let's take a manageable case. If the theory is that in a closed system, temperature and pressure are directly related (they go up or down together), then we can predict that if we increase the temperature of this specific closed system the pressure will increase. The second sentence says something such as: the temperature was increased and the pressure did not increase. Using the modus tollens argument form, one can conclude that the original theory about the relationship between temperature and pressure must be incorrect. The theory is refuted.

This example shows us why prediction is often discussed within scientific contexts. Theories commit themselves to certain specific consequences. When these consequences are checked out, we generate evidence for or against the theory. Note that there is an asymmetry in Popper's view of evidence. He argued that theories can be refuted by specific cases, but when the consequences checked out, as it were, we could not claim the theory was true with the same degree of certainty. To understand this, we must consider a logical fallacy that is close in form to modus tollens.

If this x is an A, then it is a B.
This x is a B.

Therefore, this x is an A.

This conclusion does not follow; the argument takes an invalid form. If the ball is red, then it is colorful. The ball is colorful. Therefore, the ball is red. The ball could be yellow and hot pink. The argument form affirms the consequent, and then tries to affirm the antecedent. This form is known as the fallacy of the "affirmation of the consequent." Popper argued that traditional conceptions of science committed just this fallacy. A prediction was made based on the theory. If the prediction was found to be true, the claim was that the theory was some how confirmed or supported by the evidence that the prediction was true. This led to the general notion that science was advanced by refutations of theories.

To exist as a believable theory, the theory had to pass or survive severe tests. It had to escape refutation. Theories that could endure in spite of serious attempts at refutation, were the theories that gave direction to scientific inquiry, on Popper's view.

Popper's falsifiability view of scientific logic provides us with a useful insight. How can we distinguish between serious inquiry or research, and political or ideological claims? In other words, how do we know that a given collection of "researchers" is not sorting through the evidence and reporting to us anything that supports the theory? Political groups or movements do this all the time.

Popper's view gives us an out. If we examine the process that generated the evidence, do we find that the researchers looked in all the safe places, or did they subject the claim to great risk by seeking out the most severe tests possible? In a word, did anyone attempt to falsify the claim? This question is both revealing and depressing. We can see that the notion of falsifiability provides us with an objective basis to claim that science is not subjective and arbitrary. The depressing side of the notion is that one finds so few of the committed willing to take such risks. Becoming emotionally committed to a set of beliefs actually works against truth seeking. But scientists have emotions and many times want their favorite theory to be true; so, is such objectivity possible? A small thought experiment will make this more clear. Think of something you believe—about how women are treated, about the moral adequacy of bussing, about whether taxes should be raised, and so forth. Now imagine that you walk through the library and you see the New York Times being placed on the newspaper holder. The headline is something such as, "Million Dollar Government Study Shows that . . . " Insert there a positive statement of your belief. Ask yourself how you feel. If you feel a great sense of fulfillment, then it would be better for you not to research this topic—at least until you could achieve a detached attitude.

Popper's view continues to have great influence in the literature. For example, many concerned with the development of an account of evolutionary epistemology have used his view as an analytical framework.[46] Falsifiability and the notion of nonsurvival have an obvious relationship. There are two objections to Popper's theory of scientific rationality. On the one hand, when a theory or hypothesis passes or survives a serious attempt to falsify it, Popper recognizes that the theory has achieved something more than it had prior to testing. He uses the term "corroboration" for this something more. Some think however, that the notion of corroboration is little more than the basic empiricist conception of confirmation—the degree of confidence we may have in a theory, given a set of confirming data.[47] On the other hand, some think that Popper's view and its sole commitment to falsifiability is too strong, because in the development of any theory there will be stages along the way that will produce discrepancies with known data, and therefore, the theory will be judged false prematurely.[48]

This was Lakatos's judgment as well. With respect to his metamethodology, Lakatos felt that "in my conception criticism does not—and must not—kill as fast as Popper imagined."[49] Lakatos thought that falsifiability might well stop a research program long before it can receive a full evaluation. Research programs always hit rough spots; methodological falsificationism may be too harsh or strict a master by not providing some degree of error before being considered a complete failure. Falsifiability seems to be very clean and tidy logically and does, in a sense, capture the rationality of scientific research. But is science rational in this way? Or, is science in fact less rational than this view suggests? Popper has found a way to fit deductive methods to scientific research, but it must be added that this is a reconstructed fitting, because as Kuhn argues, the actual conduct of science does not reflect this methodology.

Popperian falsifiability theory does emphasize the important role falsification plays in science, but it too tightly ties its warrant to a rule of deductive inference. Is modus tollens the best formal structure to which we can appeal? The Bayesians think not.

Bayesian Inference

The Bayesian approach to characterizing and justifying scientific inference derives from the use of Bayes's theorem in probability theory, a theorem studied by every student in an introductory course in probability theory. The theorem allows one to take an initial or "prior probability," a given set of data or evidence, and then produce by means of the theorem, a "posterior probability." Bayes's theorem is a fundamental part of elementary probability theory and presents us with a formal account of *how probabilities change given specific evidence*. A leading advocate of the Bayesian approach, Wesley Salmon, summarizes this view as follows:

> Bayes' theorem casts considerable light upon the logic of scientific inference. It provides a coherent schema in terms of which we can understand the roles of confirmation, falsification, corroboration, and plausibility. It yields a theory of scientific inference that unifies such apparently irreconcilable views as the

standard hypothetical-deductive theory, Popper's deductivism, and Hanson's logic of discovery.[50]

One of the main objections to the Bayesian interpretation of inductive inference concerned the selection of the prior probabilities. How do we determine the actual values for our prior probabilities? Some have thought that we could select our priors more or less arbitrarily. That is, if two people begin with different beliefs about the probability of some event such as an earthquake in Saint Louis, the more data that is generated, the more the posterior probabilities would approach each other. The difference in the posterior probabilities produced from each person's prior probabilities and the evidence will converge as the evidence accumulates. If the potential for generating any amount of evidence is greater than the initial differences in belief among researchers, then we do not have to worry about beliefs at the origin of research. What we have to do is to create much evidence. But what is to stop one from examining the posterior probability that is created from the evidence and one's initial belief, and then concluding that one must have been wrong about one's choice of prior probabilities? This objection involves more than simply worrying about those who would force the result they wanted by changing their prior beliefs. Re-examining our beliefs in light of the evidence is usually taken to be open-minded. But if the use of the theorem leads us to change our priors, then do we have a legitimate form of inference? If one variable in the equation is arbitrary, then the resulting posterior probabilities are just as arbitrary. This point has led some to speak of "Salmon's subjective solution" to the problem of induction—which is misleading in that the expression shades out the role being played by objective evidence.

There is no doubt that the Bayesian interpretation of scientific research is the most highly refined version that empiricism has produced and does reconstruct and clarify earlier accounts of inductive inference. It is, no doubt, the high-water mark of logical empiricism versus Hume. But, as I will argue in chapter 5, using a mathematical theorem hardly justifies the analytic conception of a priori knowledge in science. Mathematically changing probabilities in light of specific quantified evidence does not refute alternative conceptions of the role of the a priori in scientific thought.

Summary for Teachers

These two versions of contemporary methodological foundationism can be useful to teachers as they think about the nature of belief and evidence. There is much talk in the teaching literature about constructivism, the view that meaning cannot be created by teachers and transmitted to students because it is the students who must construct meaning for themselves. Popper's theory suggests that a valid approach to constructivist teaching is to challenge the patterns of meaning that students construct. Teachers can point students in directions where their ideas will be subjected to evaluation by the known evidence, but in other cases, they might ask directly: What type of evidence would falsify your theory? Or, what type of evidence would tend to count against your theory? Some might respond by saying (and some people have actually done so) that there can be no such evidence because the theory (they are defending) is true. They are saying that they cannot imagine any falsifying conditions for their views, which leads us to think that their views are functioning for them as analytic truths. Unrefutable truths are analytic in that they must be true no matter what our world turns out to be. But such truths, as the empiricists point out, can tell us nothing about our world. What we have are, in a sense, empty truths. So, if our claims are not functioning analytically for us, then it is always pertinent to ask about the nature of falsifying evidence.

The criticism of falsifiability theory is also instructive for teachers. The concern was that falsification is so harsh a master that ideas that may require considerable refinement before they would be accepted may be abandoned too quickly if any negative evidence appears. At times teachers may have to encourage students to stay with their ideas and not to give up just because everything is not going as desired.

Salmon's theory presents a way of upgrading our beliefs on the basis of evidence. In other words, no matter what views of our world we embrace, it is always possible to have this view changed by actual evidence about the world. And if Salmon is correct in his claim that his Bayesian theory subsumes Popper's theory, then Salmon's account of how we can rationally change our beliefs on the evidence available to us is as adequate an account as empiricism has achieved. For teachers, Bayesian inference means that whatever beliefs students hold as they begin an inquiry will be changed as the inquiry progresses and actually converge, given enough time and data.

The arguments against methodological foundationism are also suggestive for teachers. If it is a mistake to attempt to separate psychology from the study of the logical structures upon which knowledge is based, and if it is also a mistake to attempt to establish the logical structure of knowledge *before* any appeals to experience, then our ideas about how best to approach teaching may be in need of revision. For example, the notion that the study of an academic area should begin with learning the definitions of key terms is mistaken. The basic logical structure is not established before any appeals to students' experiences in the area of study. As we will see in chapter 4, the problem of defining central terms often comes after experience has been analyzed. In a sense, students must draw from their own experiences to establish what words mean.

3

HOW MUCH CAN WE LEARN
FROM EVERYDAY TALK?

THE PRECEDING CHAPTER presented the empiricists' view of a priori knowledge. Before we turn to the question of the other ways that a priori knowledge has been characterized by philosophers, I would like to pause to consider another aspect of philosophic analysis. As we have seen, First Philosophy generated a view of what it means to do conceptual analysis, but there is another view of how conceptual analysis can be put to work in education. In chapter 4, we will return to the issue of the nature of a priori knowledge.

What Is Ordinary Language Analysis?

Within the literature of philosophy of education, the justification for the way that language analysis was practiced was not limited to First Philosophy and its search for rational meaning apart from human experience. The methodology of language analysis developed by (as philosophers say) "the later Wittgenstein," or the Wittgenstein of *Philosophical Investigations*,[1] moved away from First Philosophy and became what is now known as *ordinary language analysis* because it took seriously language in everyday use. On this view of the methodology of conceptual analysis, the meaning of words is still regarded as existing prior to what individuals do with them, but the method of establishing such meanings is changed from rational philosophic reflection to the analysis of how words serve us in ordinary or everyday language. As Stanley Cavell remarked, "I know of no respectable philosopher since the time of Descartes who entrusts the health of the human spirit to ordinary language with Wittgenstein's completeness."[2]

The First Philosophy view of language analysis did not see ordinary language as being especially valuable for philosophers. Attempts to provide a rational foundation for scientific inference and theory choice, for example, made no appeals to everyday meanings because it was assumed that ordinary meanings would be reconstructed to present a consistent account of scientific knowledge. Even the language used by scientists was seen as little more than a starting point for rational reconstruction. As Nelson Goodman claims, "Scientists and philosophers often . . . trim and patch the use of ordinary terms to suit their special needs, deviating from popular usage even where it is quite unambiguous."[3] While philosophers of science rejected ordinary language analysis, it flourished in other areas of philosophy. For example, during the 1970s there was a great concern for the meaning of 'intention', and those ordinary-language characteristics that remain the same in all its uses.[4]

Wittgenstein of the *Investigations* views language in a much more bleak fashion. Cavell makes several telling observations. "The *Investigations* lends itself to, perhaps it calls out for, competing emphases in its consideration of human discourse—an emphasis on its distrust of language or an emphasis on its trust of ordinary human speech. The competition is the emblem of philosophy's struggle with itself."[5] Cavell finds philosophers coming down on different sides of this trust issue as they understand Wittgenstein. He observes that the Wittgenstein of First Philosophy held (in the *Tractatus*) that the propositions of ordinary language are "in perfect logical order" (5.5563). "But that order is exactly not, as I would like to say it is for the *Investigations*, recognized as the medium of philosophical thinking. The power of this recognition of the ordinary for philosophy is bound up with the recognition that refusing or forcing the order of the ordinary is a cause of philosophical emptiness (say avoidance) and violence."[6] There is no doubt that logical empiricism's emphasis on rational reconstruction of concepts was a forcing of order on the ordinary. Cavell continues:

> When Wittgenstein finds that "philosophy is a battle against the bewitchment of our intelligence by means of language" . . . he is not as I understand him there naming language simply (perhaps not at all) as the efficient cause of philosophical grief, but as the medium of its dispelling. One may perhaps speak of language and its form of life—the human—as a standing opportunity for grief (as if we are spoiling for grief) for which language is the relief. The weapon is put into our hands, but we *need* not turn it on ourselves. What turns it upon us is philosophy, the desire for thought, running out of control. That has become an inescapable fate for us, apparently accompanying the fate of having human language.[7]

We must be careful with language and not allow use to become abuse. It was Locke who noted that some philosophers threw dust into the air and then complained about not being able to see.

Wittgenstein was concerned that, by using symbolic logic as the medium of rational reconstruction, we were playing fast and loose with language, to our eventual peril. (The empiricist literature around midcentury made extensive use of symbolic logic, especially predicate calculus.) Many philosophers working today have come to share his concern. In a sense, Wittgenstein of the *Investigations* is a naturalist who sees everyday language as a part of a living, organic corpus rather than as a reflection of underlying formal symbolic structure.

But are there dangers in relying too heavily on ordinary meanings? Appeals to ordinary language meanings tend to be theoretically conservative.[8] Cavell reports that Russell viewed the *Investigations* as an expression of "*petit bourgeois* fear of change, whether of individual inventiveness or of social revolution."[9] While Wittgenstein sees philosophy as leaving everything as it is, the pursuers of rational arguments found it much easier to deconstruct existing meanings.

There has recently emerged another line of argumentation that amounts to a direct attack on the methodology of ordinary language analysis. Because the Gettier counterexamples cast serious doubt on the idea of an epistemology free of the findings of psychological research, another group of philosophers is arguing for a much more radical view of the role of cognitive science in theory of knowledge. The Churchlands,[10] who refer to themselves as "eliminative materialists" because they believe that psychology can be eliminated in favor of material studies of the form and function of neural tissue, center their argument around the claim that common-sense psychology, now known in the philosophic literature as folk psychology, stands in the way of further developing our understanding of mental processes such as intentions, consciousness, and knowing.

What Is Folk Psychology?

Patricia Churchland's concerns have much in common with those of educational psychology. "What we want to know is how humans and other animals learn, what makes them smart, how they plan and problem solve, how they recollect and forget, how their brains differ when their personalities differ, how they can be self-aware, what consciousness is."[11] As she sees it, the only way to obtain an adequate account of these phenomena is to put the findings of neuroscience to work in epistemology, ultimately constructing a "theoretical unification of neuroscience and psychology."[12]

Many radical naturalists believe that a major obstacle to the search for this account is folk psychology, and they want to eliminate it from cognitive science, believing that neuroscience is a better source of the explanations sought. Moreover, if folk psychology is incorrect and an inadequate framework for thinking about how we learn, feel, and solve problems, then this calls into question the status of ordinary language analysis as a method in philosophy of education. This question alone makes the consideration of the epistemological foundations of folk psychology important.

What is folk psychology, and why do the radical naturalists find it so objectionable? Patricia Churchland has presented fairly complete arguments in this regard.

> Now by folk psychology I mean that rough-hewn set of concepts, generalizations, and rules of thumb we all standardly use in explaining and predicting human behavior. Folk psychology is common-sense psychology—the psychological lore in virtue of which we explain behavior as the outcome of beliefs, desires, perceptions, expectations, goals, sensations, and so forth. It is a theory whose generalizations connect mental states to other mental states, to perceptions, and to actions. These homey generalizations are what provide the characterization of the mental states and processes referred to; they are what delimit the "facts" of mental life and define the explananda. Folk psychology is intuitive "psychology," and it shapes our conceptions of ourselves. As philosophers have analyzed it, the preeminent elements in folk psychological explanations of behavior include the concepts of *belief* and *desire*. Other elements will of course figure in, but these two are crucial and indispensable.[13]

In the dark past we can imagine early humans using their intelligence to survive and prosper. Learning to predict environmental events has survival value, and developing ideas about what others might do in various situations would also be useful. The phenomenology of self-consciousness and the stimulus-generalizing projection of beliefs and intentions on other people must somehow be involved in the rise of a set of concepts and principles by which observable behavior is explained—two million years later to be named 'folk psychology.'

The everyday language of any culture across time and space contains the folk wisdom of that culture. The debate over folk psychology focuses on the status of these ideas. Patricia Churchland has doubts about the value of folk psychology, for as she notes, "it would be astonishing if folk psychology, alone among the folk theories, was essentially correct."[14] What are the other folk theories? She frequently mentions folk physics, but let us consider it from an independent source.

Reinders Duit describes the responses of students and others who are shown a drawing of the path of a ball thrown through the air.[15] The drawing shows the ball at the top of its arc and the subjects are asked to draw the force or forces acting on the ball. Subjects without university education commonly show two forces: gravity with downward arrow and the direction of the path of the ball with another arrow. They think this second force is required to pull the ball along its path. Duit explains: "Our daily experiences with pulling and pushing of bodies support the idea that whenever a body has to be kept in motion a force in the direction of the motion is needed. However, this is not true from the Newtonian point of view."[16]

The two-force-theory respondents agree with Aristotle that an object will remain in motion as long as a force is applied to it. The catapult presented a difficulty. When the projectile left the catapult, there was no longer a force being applied to it, yet it continued in motion. To explain this observation, the impetus theory was generated. The projectile was given impetus by the catapult. This impetus gradually dissipated and the projectile fall back to earth. "A corollary to the theory was that objects could be given curved impetus, so that an object twirled around the end of a string allegedly continued in a circular path when released from the string."[17]

The familiar can be a hindrance to insight. As Patricia Churchland argues,

> Although folk psychology has a profound familiarity and obviousness, and although the categories of folk psychology are observationally applied, it nevertheless remains true that folk psychology is a theoretical framework and hence a framework whose adequacy can be questioned and assessed. The adequacy of folk psychology is in no way secured by its seeming to be overwhelmingly obvious, by it being observationally applied, by its being applied introspectively, or even by its being innate, if such be the case. If we see that folk psychology has no right to epistemological privilege, and no immunity to revision and correction, then we can begin to see that its generalizations and categories can be corrected and improved upon. Indeed, an underlying theme in scientific psychology is that they can and are being modified and even superseded.[18]

The claim that folk psychology might just be like folk physics must be taken seriously. Will there come a time when students read about folk psychology and shake their heads the way we do when we read about impetus physics? The only reliable way to deal with these matters is to review the facts and the frameworks that give them meaning. Churchland is explicit on the parallel between folk physics and folk psychology. "Just as it turned out that there was no such thing as impetus, there may be no such thing as awareness. This is not as bizarre as it first sounds. Presumably there is *some* monitoring mechanism or other chugging away in the mind-brain in virtue of which our current employment of the concept of 'awareness' can get a foothold—just as there is something or other going on in the world in virtue of which the employment of the concept 'impetus' got a foothold."[19] Her analogical argument should give us pause. The point is that we should be very careful about the framework we use to understand our cognitive and affective states. We have to be open to the fact that folk psychology is, as she puts it, "so misconceived, and its taxonomy so askew, that even the formulation of our questions thwarts our inquiry."[20]

Dennett seems to be in agreement: "If we individuate states (beliefs, states of consciousness, states of communicative intention, etc.) by their content—which is the standard means of individuation in folk psychology—we end up having to postulate differences that are systematically undiscoverable by any means, from the inside or the outside, and in the process, we lose the subjective intimacy or incorrigibility that is supposedly the hallmark of consciousness."[21] Dennett is doing more than questioning the adequacy of the framework provided by folk psychology for understanding mental phenomena; his suggestion that this framework renders certain aspects of learning and cognition "systematically undiscoverable" means that adopting folk psychology as a basis for thinking is self-defeating.

Ordinary Language Analysis in Philosophy of Education

The conceptual analysts in education attempt to clarify the meanings of words used in the description and justification of school policies and teaching practices. It is not assumed by ordinary English language philosophers that everyday discourse contains all the knowledge and wisdom that is required to operate schools, only that it is through a careful analysis of the everyday meanings of the language used to think about schools, that we can come to better formulations of the problems faced by educators; through analysis, we will not be misled by fuzzy meanings and equivocal thinking.

In the study of education, the methodology of ordinary language analysis was focused on establishing the meanings of terms such as 'education', 'teaching' and 'learning' as the meanings of these terms are of obvious import for thinking about educational theory and teacher conduct. Within philosophy of education there was no antagonism or even much of a distinction to be drawn between rational analysis and ordinary language analysis. As noted, many of Scheffler's educational writings are clear examples of rational analysis, and there are explicit cases of ordinary language analyses of 'teaching', for example, within the literature.[22] Within these two methodological limits, we find most of the analytic literature in philosophy of education, which, as I said, is not particularly concerned with this methodological distinction. From an analysis of everyday meanings of words used to talk about education, discussions could move easily to rational arguments.

Ordinary language meanings are normative; as Paul Churchland argues, the reason we ascribe normative force to the principles of folk psychology is because we value most of these principles. We take folk psychology to be the ideal of rationality, which makes it not only an explanation of what we do, but a standard or norm for conduct and interpretations of what others do.[23] An ordinary language analysis of the term 'teaching' is an investigation of the relevant normative principles. Such analyses are not as passively accepting of extant language as readers might suspect. As Gilbert Ryle pointed out, analysts do not simply report meanings as they are found in ordinary language, but they consider normative criteria for the use of terms—they "rectify" what we already know, as he put it.[24] This involves norms beyond those found in folk psychology or the canonical structure of ordinary language.

Let's be true to the literature on this point. Some philosophers have tried to stay within the bounds of ordinary language, which means that they gave it normative force and did not see themselves as rectifying its meanings. Within the analysis of educational discourse, some analyses have drawn their legitimation from ordinary meanings. My point is that the more closely an analysis remains to the canonical structure of ordinary language, the more it encounters the criticism of the Churchlands.

Ryle's notion of the rectification of ordinary language avoids this criticism, but it points us to the question of what normative criteria should be used in the process. These criteria come from the methodology of First Philosophy. The naturalists' discontent with this view of conceptual analysis is that it is not epistemically possible to establish an a priori in an inquiry that is independent of scientific research. In philosophy of education there continue to be extensive discussions of what it means to teach in a rational manner or to be a rational person. These discussions seldom if ever appeal to scientific theories. In this, I believe that they are instantiations of the methodology of First Philosophy. These discussions of rationality present an example of my concern. Can we adequately write about rationality without considering scientific findings? Furthermore, how could results of psychological and biological studies of human nature not be relevant to the basic frameworks in light of which we study worthwhile teaching, rational curriculum development, and other efforts to influence the cognitive and emotional development of children? All too many of our colleagues in education believe that philosophy of education is irrelevant to the problems faced by educational researchers and practitioners. It turns out that many of our philosophic colleagues are making the same point.

Robert Heslep, in his presidential address to the Philosophy of Education Society, concluded, "a theory of mind in analytical philosophy of education might provide a framework from within which research in educational psychology might be conducted."[25] This is an example of post-Fregean conceptual analysis. Analytical philosophy of education on this view, establishes norms for the meanings and relationships of mentalistic terms contained in educational discourse prior to scientific investigation in psychology and neuroscience. But as Robert E. McCauley argues, "Philosophical speculation about the capacity, processing, development, and organization of our cognitive system uninformed by the achievements in these sciences risks thoroughgoing irrelevance to what systematic knowledge we have about these matters."[26] Whatever one believes about the potential of conceptual analysis for education, there is reason to believe that now is a time for reevaluation.

Some of the best conceptual analyses focused on the concept of teaching, and several of the best of these are contained in a collection of essays entitled *Concepts of Teaching*.[27] In their introductory essay, Macmillan and Nelson compare conceptual analysis of teaching with studies that observed actual classroom behavior, which were popular at that time.[28] "In sharp contrast with these . . . approaches to studying teaching is the small movement that tries to get clear what is or might be *meant* when we speak of someone as teaching something. It is one thing to report (classify, count) what teachers *do* when they are in the classroom and quite another to say how we know that what they are doing is rightly *called* teaching. Put yet differently: What is the correct (or defensible) concept of teaching? And given such a concept, what denotations fall under it?"[29]

Some researchers observed hundreds of teachers in their classrooms in an attempt to answer the question, "What is teaching?" but the conceptual analysts asked the "prior question,"[30] namely, what does the word 'teaching' mean? The researchers who observed and classified teachers' verbal behavior had to begin with some sort of working definition of teaching—what people called teachers do in places called classrooms. The conceptual analysts, by contrast, investigated the established language to extricate the meanings involved. In a sense, conceptual analysis sought to produce a definition of 'teaching' by establishing the proper criteria or conditions that compose the *definiens* ('teaching' is the *definiendum*). I say "in a sense" because the concept of definition is itself controversial.[31] Years ago, I tried to show that by paying attention to the methodology of definition we could contribute to the development of educational discourse, but empiricistic language analysis was so entrenched at that time that there was no interest in that methodology. My distinction between right-handed defining (the analysis of existing terms) and left-handed defining (the insertion of new terms into technical discourse) is important.[32] As long as we do not think of definitions as stipulative or arbitrary, there is no problem created by thinking that conceptual analysis aims at definition. (Skeptics do claim that if we laid all the conceptual analysts end-to-end they would not reach a definition.)

The problem for the methodology of conceptual analysis that emerges from the thinking of the Churchlands, among others, is one of the epistemic status of the results of ordinary language analysis. The resource or raw material for conceptual analysis is contained in ordinary language. Conceptual analysis identifies and refines ordinary language meanings, a process that leads us into folk psychology. In the analyses of 'teaching' there is reference to intentions. In my own analysis of 'studying' I tried to show that studying is intentional learning.[33] The meaning of 'intention', as it appears in the analyses of 'teaching' is not unrelated to the meaning of 'consciousness'. We analyzed 'teaching', 'learning', 'studying' and so forth in terms of the mentalistic elements of ordinary language meanings, which took these analyses into folk psychology. If we claim that conceptual analysis goes well beyond ordinary language meanings, then what is the epistemological status of this additional methodology?

This situation must give us pause because, soon after Frege's work in conceptual analysis, philosophers wondered if many of the problems pursued by traditional philosophy were not a function of the poor language being used to express them. Dennett and the Churchlands can be seen as wondering the same thing about what we have been up to. Their wonderings are not simply a further refinement of the conceptual analysis of mentalistic terms; their wonderings are about its elimination. I see no way to screen off the criticism that to the degree that we use the meanings of ordinary language in our analyses we are engaged in the analysis of folk psychological concepts. If folk psychology is an inadequate psychology that leads us to misframe the questions we ask, as

Dennett and the Churchlands suggest, then we have a methodological problem crying out for attention.

These arguments raise methodological questions about attempting to see philosophy of education as the analysis of ordinary language as a means of establishing the meaning of educational terms such as 'teaching', 'learning', 'explaining' among others. If the epistemic status of the framework we use to think about our psychological nature is no better than that of folk physics, then studies of ordinary language concepts about child rearing, instructing, teaching, and so forth are suspect because of their folk psychological roots. The tradition that gave rise to the methodology of ordinary language analysis has not attended to these discussions, which are debates mainly between the radical and the traditional naturalists. Twenty years ago my criticism of ordinary language analysis was that it did not pay enough attention to either (a) the goals (sometimes called epistemic utilities) of scientific research, or (b) its findings. "Analysis of terms such as 'learning,' 'teaching,' etc., are very often conducted in such a way that neither the best empirical knowledge nor the epistemic utilities are taken into account."[34] We have seen that both First Philosophy and ordinary language analysis are prevented by their methodological assumptions from considering scientific research in their analyses. But the consequence is that this inattention to scientific discoveries renders language analysis a conservative force in educational discourse. Recall Russell's comment about the ordinary language analysts' "*petit bourgeois* fear of change."

Finally, Hilary Putnam has claimed that arguments such as the Churchlands' are self-defeating. In a section of *Realism and Reason*, Putnam asks, "Why not eliminate the normative from our conceptual vocabulary? Could it be a superstition that there is such a thing as reason?" His questions are in reaction to Quine, but they obviously pertain to the arguments of the epistemological naturalists as well. Putnam argues that "The elimination of the normative is attempted mental suicide." If we do engage in thinking, but convince ourselves that we cannot think, then could we just quit thinking? Putnam asks, "why should we expend our mental energy in convincing ourselves that we aren't thinkers, that our thoughts aren't really *about* anything? . . . This is a self-refuting enterprise if there ever was one!"[35]

The Naturalists' Disagreement over Folk Psychology

Radical naturalists, such as the Churchlands, argue for a complete abandonment of folk psychology on the grounds that our entrenched, traditional ways of thinking about cognition are just not up to the task of advancing the scientific study of learning. Other, less radical naturalists (what I call the traditional naturalists) take a different view of folk psychology. As naturalists, they reject First Philosophy's approach to cognitive science, but they argue that folk psychology has some value for cognitive studies.

Bruner's Defense of Folk Psychology

Jerome S. Bruner claims that while the general notion of folk psychology was "conceived in derision by the new cognitive scientists for its hospitality toward such intentional states as beliefs, desires, and meanings,"[36] it is, nevertheless, an excellent source of understanding about human thinking, and he strongly objects to those who want to view thinking as a mechanical, computational process.

> It was inevitable that with computation as the metaphor of the new cognitive science and with computability as the necessary if not sufficient criterion of a workable theory of mind within the new science, the old malaise about mentalism would reemerge. With mind equated to program, what should the status of mental states be—old fashion mental states identifiable not by their programmatic characteristics in a computational system but by their subjective marking? There could be no place for "mind" in such a system—"mind" in the sense of intentional states like believing, desiring, intending, grasping a meaning. The cry soon rose to ban such intentional states from the new science. And surely no book ever published even in the heyday of early behaviorism could match the antimentalistic zeal of Stephen Stich's *From Folk Psychology to Cognitive Science.*[37]

By his reference to computation in psychology, Bruner is pointing to the claim made by many cognitive scientists that brain processes are actually computational processes. This whole issue requires much more conceptual analysis than it has yet received. (See the remarks of John Searle in chapter 1.) Computers can deal with alphabetical information as easily as they deal with numeric data. Much of the research in artificial intelligence is concerned with writing programs that can process ordinary language. Programming languages have rules for identifying and manipulating any letter or "string" of letters. There actually exists an algebra of sentences. This, I believe, has given new life to the notion that the syntax of language can be meaningfully separated from its semantics. Armed with dictionaries, grammatical rules, and a list of common idiomatic expressions, computers can take many strings and semantically interpret them in ways that one almost forgets one is not interacting with a human being. This goes far beyond "word processing."

It is an obvious question to be asked, especially when one has had such cyber-interactive experiences: "Are our brains receiving string input and processing string data just as our computers are?" If not, what else could possibly be going on among the synapses? Some claim that this area of language processing is not open to our consciousness. In other words, we cannot experience this string processing and know of it only by inference.

For Bruner, to understand thinking, one must understand how experiences and actions are influenced by intentional states. Moreover, "the form of these intentional states is realized only through participation in the symbolic systems of the culture." The only way to study and know about intentional states is through "cultural systems of interpretation." Culture is the solvent or medium in which intentions, beliefs, and desires exist and interact. Culture is "constitutive of mind" in that through "actualization in culture, meaning achieves a form that is public and communal rather than private and autistic."[38]

Bruner cites three reasons for considering cultural analysis as a part of psychological research.

1. It is man's participation *in* culture and the realization of his mental powers *through* culture that make it impossible to construct a human psychology on the basis of the individual alone. . . .

2. By virtue of participation in culture, meaning is rendered *public* and *shared.* Our culturally adapted way of life depends upon shared meanings and shared concepts and depends as well upon shared modes of discourse for negotiating differences in meaning and interpretation. . . .

3. The power of . . . "folk psychology" . . . is a culture's account of what makes humans tick. It includes a theory of mind, one's own and others, a theory of motivation, and the rest.[39]

Infants enter into a preexisting culture and therein must find their way. It is within this medium that one has to express oneself, come to understand others, and ultimately discover who one is. Central to these processes is the phenomenon of narration. Bruner's analysis of meaning and intentional states, by means of the concept of narration, offers insights into the individual-culture relationship. But the significance of his analysis of the narrative is found in his hypothesis that children come into the world with "a readiness or predisposition to organize experience into a narrative form, into plot structures and the rest."[40]

Bruner submits several characteristics of narration. One prominent feature of the narrative is "its inherent sequentiality: a narrative is composed of a unique sequence of events, mental states, happenings involving human beings as characters or actors." Another feature of the narrative is its "indifference to extralinguistic reality."[41] That is, when one tells a story its truth or fiction does not affect it as a narrative. A third important characteristic of narration is that "it specializes in the forging of links between the exceptional and the ordinary."[42] These links are forged in terms of intentional states, desires, goals, and beliefs. The whole point of the narrative is "*to find an intentional state that mitigates or at least makes comprehensible a deviation from a canonical cultural pattern*" (emphasis in original).[43] The narrative also "reiterates the norms of the society without being didactic."[44]

Bruner's emphasis on culture and how children initiate themselves into it comes very close to Cavell's view of Wittgenstein (and who among us has a better one?):

> The *Investigations* is a work that begins with a scene of inheritance, the child's inheritance of language; it is an image of a culture as an inheritance, one that takes place, as is fundamental to Freud, in the conflict of voices and generations. The figure of the child is present in this portrait of civilization more prominently and decisively than in any other work of philosophy I can think of (with the exception, if you grant that it is philosophy, of *Emile*). It discovers or rediscovers childhood for philosophy (the child in us). . . . [45]

The child's inheritance of language is not a matter of DNA but of culture. As children learn to construct narrations of their experience, they learn of the conflict of voices and generations and add and subtract culture. As a naturalist, I certainly can think of another philosopher who put the "figure of the child" in his "portrait of civilization" as "prominently and decisively" as "any other work of philosophy." The fact that Cavell could not think of him says much about the gulf between preanalytic and analytic thought.

The most underregarded dimension of folk psychology for Bruner is the notion that, "At their core, all folk psychologies contain a surprisingly complex notion of an agentive self."[46] Bruner thinks that the glitter of computing, information processing, and artificial intelligence have "diverted" cognitive science from "its originating impulse."[47] His conception of folk psychology is "a system by which people organize their experience in, knowledge about, and transactions with the social world."[48] Note that his reference to the "social world" allows for a separation of folk psychology from folk physics.

If Patricia Churchland were to ask Bruner why he thinks that folk psychology is a true theory when all of the other folk theories have been shown to be false, his answer would seem to be that cultural traditions reflect principles of social development. Bruner, as would Quine, finds eliminative materialism too radical because it undervalues our semantic endowment. Consider Kitcher's observation: "To use a recurrent Quinean formulation, all such knowledge-generating processes are dependent on our absorption of ancestral lore, so that we are always implicitly dependent on the struggles of our predecessors to fashion a language apt for the description of the world, and are thus, vicariously, dependent on their experiences."[49] This again indicates the theme in pragmatism to ground the a priori in human experience, including ancestral experience.

McCauley's Ineliminability Argument

McCauley has criticized the elimination thesis for folk psychology because, he claims, it is based on an inadequate view of theoretical reduction.[50]

> The model of intertheoretic relations implicit in this alternative account does not preclude the elimination of folk psychology, it simply predicts that if folk psychology is eliminated, it will not be from the neuroscientific level of analysis that we should expect its likely successor. In all probability the neurosciences will share some responsibility in the crime, but it is much more likely to be some descendant of contemporary cognitive psychology that will do the actual dirty work. Consequently, this *is not* to deny Patricia Churchland's prediction that future psychology and neuroscience are likely to substantially co-evolve, but, rather, to emphasize that the language of co-evolution is a welcome corrective to the Churchlands' talk of eliminative materialism, especially since they employ both."[51]

McCauley holds that even if folk psychology can be eliminated within scientific psychology, it will not be so eliminated from ordinary language.

The analyses of McCauley and Bruner converge on the point that it would not be a good thing to eliminate folk psychology because folk psychology is a source of insight for psychologists. As McCauley states:

> Not only is an elimination of folk psychology along the lines the Churchlands' predict unlikely, it is undesirable. Maintaining the integrity of separate ana-

lytical levels in science is important to scientific progress. If cognitive psychology were to collapse into cognitive neurobiology or even to be driven by it in the way that the Churchlands' sometimes seem to expect, we would sacrifice important sources of theoretical and problem solving inspiration (currently supplied by psychological research) as well as numerous funds of evidential support at the altar of a unified, but impoverished, science.[52]

This statement reflects a theme in traditional naturalism: experience always has an emergent quality about it that is never fully predictable. To view cognition as open to analysis on multiple levels allows for several domains from which new relationships may present themselves. Like Quine and Bruner, McCauley is concerned that undue reliance on one level of analysis, neuroscience, will lead us to ignore other levels, such as our ancestral wisdom. This thinking should not, however, lead philosophers away from asking how cognitive science and neuroscience relate to epistemology. "Nor should those who champion either folk psychology, or ordinary language analysis, or the preeminence of intuition find much comfort here. None of the considerations raised . . . undermine Quine's fundamental insight that once we are bereft of appeals to First Philosophy, it is the standards of those pursuits that contribute most obviously and most successfully to human flourishing generally and to our knowledge about the world in particular that offer the clearest and most defensible standards of rational justification."[53] This raises further questions about the nature of conceptual analysis as it was practiced in philosophy of education during the analytic period.

The notion that conceptual questions can be settled *prior to* scientific questions reflects belief in one or more of the following: First Philosophy, ordinary language analysis, or analysis as the explication of our intuitions. Philosophy of education of the third millennium must find a way to incorporate scientific results into its methodology. My claim is that when First Philosophy is removed from the table, we will see that traditional pragmatism can show us the way. McCauley continues: "I assume that it is non-controversial that science deserves a prominent, if not the most prominent, position among the candidate activities. Standards that are *simultaneously external to, superior to, and independent of* those of science simply do not exist. The standards to which scientific communities aspire and the results at which they arrive jointly constitute compelling grounds for regarding scientific endeavor as the paradigm case of rational inquiry."[54] Any philosopher of education who is at all literate in the works of John Dewey knows that the thinking that has led science to such remarkable achievements was central to Dewey's philosophy. With the current attacks on empiricism and the renewed concern for epistemological naturalism (pragmatism), Dewey's thought deserves continued attention.

Intermediate Conclusions

First Philosophy sought to establish a foundation that would support conceptual analytical inquiry by appeal to the analyticity of symbolic logic and a methodology for objective observation. A serious weakness turns out to be its rejection of any scientific content in the development of this foundation. How can rationality be set forth without attention to what we know about how we think? Ordinary language philosophy emerged, in a sense, as a reaction to First Philosophy's shoehorning all of our linguistic meaning into categories developed in light of a single goal, that is, to make discourse rational. Ordinary language philosophers hold that First Philosophy does not appreciate the holistic nature of language and its relationship to culture. In this unappreciation, philosophers have experienced self-inflicted grief. In this conclusion, the ordinary language philosophers come close to the Quine-Bruner view that we are required to attend to our semantic endowment under pain of cognitive bewilderment.

It is somewhat ironic that the radical naturalists' rejection of folk psychology is held to be a way of avoiding grief in cognitive psychological theory. Even though ordinary language philosophy respects the organic nature of natural languages, its overly conservative nature, which Cavell himself attributes to Wittgenstein, prevents it from becoming free of its own falsehoods and oversimplifications. The major criticism of ordinary language philosophy turns out to be the same one that is held against First Philosophy, that there is no provision for the incorporation of scientific findings in its analyses. Any methodology of conceptual analysis will have to come to grips with science. This is especially clear at present as we watch cognitive science dominate the concerns of epistemology. Kitcher holds that "conceptual clarification can play a valuable role within the naturalist enterprise, even though it is clearly understood that the concepts in question might be superseded."[55] The concepts could be superseded by scientific findings. The idea that an adequate methodology of conceptual analysis can be correctly applied and that the results of this analysis can be superseded by science seems to take a rather jury-rigged view of analysis. It makes more sense to me to view the methodology of conceptual analysis as already containing the wherewithal to manage or incorporate scientific findings within its analyses so that its results will be superseded only by more accurate and creative uses of that methodology. It is this strategy that I will pursue in subsequent chapters.

Before this can be attempted there emerges the following question. With all of this talk about conceptual analysis making use of scientific results, one is led to wonder: Is conceptual analysis a theoretical part of scientific analysis?

Is Conceptual Analysis Science?

In order for scientific hypotheses to avoid being true or false by definition, the variables in hypotheses must be independently definable; we require hypothetical relationships to be true or false on the data, not by definition. The classic example, "All bachelors are unmarried" is true by definition, that is, it cannot be both understood and denied. Considerations such as this involve scientific theorists in the activity of making and evaluating definitions. The question we should entertain is the following: Is this process of making and evaluating definitions in science actually what we mean by 'conceptual analysis'? Giere, for example, claims that "philosophy of science is itself a science,"[56] and if he is correct, then we have reason to wonder if conceptual analysis as done within philosophy of science is scientific activity.

But the problem cuts equally well the other way. Perhaps it is science, not philosophy, that is the bogus inquiry. There might be some reason to wonder if the empiricists were not doing science under the rubric 'philosophy', but some wonder if scientists are not doing philosophy (or worse, ideology) under the guise of science. There are those who argue that scientific knowledge is entirely a sociopolitical construction, that is, *all* aspects of what we call 'scientific knowledge' are completely of our own making. Collins, for example, states that "the natural world has a small or non-existent role in the construction of scientific knowledge."[57] Others hold that truth is what is created by the politically dominant view, even in physics.[58]

Peter Berger and Thomas Luckmann's well-known book, *The Social Construction of Reality*,[59] is sometimes taken to be an argument for the total constructivist view of science. Giere addressed this point and helps put this issue in some perspective.

> The revealing fact is that Berger and Luckmann's book is about the social construction of *social* reality. The two main chapters, in addition to the introduction and conclusion, are titled "Society as Objective Reality" and "Society as

Subjective Reality." The authors explicitly declined to pursue questions about the role of "modern science" in society. . . . And in considering relationships between biology and society, they explicitly noted that some socially conceivable projects, such as legislating that men should bear children, "would founder on the hard facts of human biology" . . . Yes, "hard facts"![60]

We may create our own Heaven or Hell, but it is species chauvinism (or even psychopathy) to claim that the extrahuman part of the universe plays no role in our view of it.

If science is no more legitimate than any other human construction, then it is only to be expected that some will raise questions about the difference between practitioners in science and practitioners in witchcraft, claiming there is no epistemological difference between the two. Some have gone so far as to claim that what we call 'science' is nothing more than "our magic."[61] What these total constructivists want to argue, as Giere notes, is "the general thesis that a society's image of the *natural* world is completely on a par with its image of the social world. Both are culturally relative, and in neither case is it possible to prove one image superior to the other."[62] Giere claims that this is just posturing: "If our goal is to understand the natural world in a way that makes modern technology possible, we simply must admit that contemporary scientific practice is superior to Azande witchcraft. The task for the cultural study of science is to explain why this is so, not to deny the obvious."[63] Conceptual analysis for the total social constructivists becomes a matter of studying what people do and what they say when they are doing it. There is no way to evaluate the adequacy of what they do and say. Put differently, there is no normative dimension to this inquiry—other than the statistical sense of 'normative'.

Laudan addressed the Edinburgh school, the view that since science is a social enterprise, science is best understood by sociological methods.[64] Laudan says that this view amounts to saying that since "syphilis is a social disease it is only or primarily the sociologists who can have scientific knowledge of syphilis." This analogy portends problems. Laudan refers to such views as pseudoscience because the adherents of the sociological view of philosophy of science are "unable or unwilling," as Laudan says, to tell us what is *scientific* about their methods.

Circular reasoning is a problem for these kinds of approaches to understanding science. Let's say that some sociologists are studying an area of scientific research such as the human genome. The results of this sociological study are scientific results, because the sociological study of science is itself a science. We could turn our attention to these sociological studies of science, attempting to determine what terms the sociologists are using and what these terms mean. Our inquiry must itself be a scientific one; we are engaged in the sociological study of the sociology of human genetics. What will we do if, during our study of the sociology of human genetics, disagreements arise about how best to study the sociology of science? We can, by hypothesis, identify nothing extrasocial to which conclusions must be true and, thus, have no non-arbitrary way to fix belief.

The problem is that the methodology of the sociological study of science is being turned on itself. We are attempting to use sociological methods to study sociological methods, but questions about methodological adequacy in sociological studies of science cannot be resolved by appeal to the methodology of sociological studies of science. This is viciously circular. When we read the published studies of the sociology of physics or psychology, what are we to make of them? What epistemic merit do they have? So the "philosophy of science is sociology of science" view undergoes a typical Humean epistemological meltdown. Attempting to see the methodology of conceptual analysis as the methodology of science does not get at the root issue: how do we give our analyses normative force?

4

THE PRAGMATIC A PRIORI

Introduction

THE BASIC PROBLEM of epistemology is scientific knowledge, and the central issue in scientific knowledge is the proper way to think about the nature and role of the a priori therein. As we have seen, empiricism is, in essence, the philosophic strategy of placing the analytic conception of the a priori, along with observation language, at the methodological center of epistemology. Many philosophers now believe that this strategy has run its course and that an alternative approach is called for. In this chapter, I want to consider what the pragmatist alternative to empiricism means for the methodology of conceptual analysis, but before we engage in this pursuit, it is worth our time to review what some refer to as Kant's a priori.

The Synthetic Conception of A Priori Knowledge

One conception of a priori knowledge originated with the German philosopher Immanuel Kant, who is significant for educators because it is his thinking that provides the basis for Jean Piaget's theory of cognitive development. Though the point is seldom recognized, Piaget explicitly rejected the empiricists' notion of a priori knowledge and set out to use Kant's conception of a priori knowledge to develop an improved way of studying child development.

David Hume's answer to the question "How do we know?" is that the mind at birth is blank, a tabula rasa, and that through sensory experience we come to know the world. This is sometimes referred to as the copy theory of knowledge because it takes knowledge acquisition to be a copying process, much as a photograph is an optical record of an instance of space-time. Kant argued that this view is mistaken in its claim that sensory information can be assimilated by the mind in a pure, uninterrupted form. Sensory data must be interpreted before it becomes sensory experience. Kant's alternative to Hume's explanation was that minds bring something to experience that does not originate in sensory experience. The mind, he claimed, possesses a specific structure that is not formed by its sensory experience but is required for having sensory experiences. For Kant, the human mind has a preestablished form. By means of innate (preformed) categories, our sensory experience is interpreted and organized.[1]

Synthetic statements are statements about the world, while analytic statements are true no matter what this world turns out to be. Logical empiricism holds that all synthetic statements are a posteriori because their truth is established by sensory experience, and all a priori knowledge is contained in analytically true statements. Kant does not disagree with the logical empiricists' view that there are analytic statements, true solely because of the rules of language; indeed he used this notion to set forth his revolutionary view. His point is that the statements that form the foundations of scientific knowledge are a priori truths, not grounded in sensory experience, that are about the world, that is, synthetic. This means that there are some a priori truths expressed in synthetic statements—synthetic a priori knowledge. This knowledge is synthetic in that it is about the world, but it is also a priori, which means that the knowledge does not come from experiencing the world. Synthetic a priori knowledge is true of the world and is independent of sensory experience. Euclidean geometry was Kant's best example. Kant claimed that the mind was prestructured to see the world in terms of Euclidean geometry. Geometric knowledge did not come from sensory experience. Geometry and other mathematical knowledge came from the mind, independent of all such experience. Recall that theorems of geometry can be proved without reference to actual measurements (what mathematicians call "metrics") or other sensory data. Deductive proofs are given for conclusions. Students do not predict how long the side of a triangle would be and then go out with a tape measure to check out the prediction. For Kant, Euclidean geometry was the only way in which we can interpret space, but this interpretation was not something we learned from experience. In other words, without Euclidean geometry we would find spatial reasoning impossible. This suggests Descartes's pronouncement, "Mathematics is the language in which God wrote the universe."

Wesley Salmon states:

According to Kant, geometry constitutes a necessary form into which our experience of objective physical reality must fit. It is a necessary form of visualization. Kant admitted the possibility of alternative types of geometry as formal toys for mathematicians to play with, but they were epistemologically unsuitable as forms for experience of the objective world. Kant claims, therefore, that Euclidean geometry, although equal to the non-Euclidean geometries from the purely logical aspect, held a privileged position from an *epistemological* standpoint.[2]

Salmon goes on to say that this view is widely held today, that many believe it is impossible to visualize physical reality in terms other than Euclidean; that is, the mind is so structured that it cannot comprehend physical space in any other terms.

Kant's epistemology has influenced scientific methodology. The great zoologists Jean Piaget and Konrad Lorenz explicitly rejected empiricism's approach to science and conducted attacks on what they saw as its mistakes.[3] Moreover, both of them explicitly embraced Kant's notion of synthetic a priori knowledge. Lorenz wrote, "The innate is not only what is not learned but what must be in existence before all individual learning in order to make learning possible. Thus, consciously paraphrasing Kant's definition of the *a priori*, we might define our concept of the innate."[4] And Piaget once commented that, "Any epistemologist reading these lines will recognize the language of Kant (except that in this case the *a priori* is a development in itself!)."[5] Piaget's research could accurately be characterized as a study of how the Kantian a priori develops from birth to maturity. By embracing this Kantian notion of synthetic a priori knowledge, both Lorenz and Piaget were directed to a set of problems different from those of empiricism and pragmatism.

Empiricists, with the possible exception of John Stuart Mill,[6] argue that mathematical knowledge is analytic and not synthetic a priori in nature.[7] As Salmon notes, the existence of non-Euclidian geometries does not refute Kant's claim that Euclidean geometry is a good example of synthetic a priori knowledge. The non-Euclidean geometries develop different meanings for fundamental geometric terms such as 'between' and 'parallel'. If one thinks of the great circles on a globe (the largest circles possible on a given sphere, called "geodesics"), it is possible to form a triangle composed of three geodesics so that all angles of that triangle are right angles.

Salmon claims that subsequent philosophic analysis of the epistemological status of geometry has shown two points.

First, the alleged inability of people to visualize non-Euclidean geometries, if such inability does obtain, is a fact of empirical psychology; it is not a necessary aspect of the human intellect that can be demonstrated philosophically. Second, the supposition that we cannot visualize non-Euclidean geometries is probably false. This false supposition is based partly upon the lack of clarity about what we mean by "visualize" and partly upon the accident of being born into a world on which Euclidean relations are frequently exemplified by physical objects (at least to a high degree of approximation) and non-Euclidean relations are not. The net effect of the analysis of geometry is a rejection of the doctrine that geometry is synthetic *a priori*. To see this, it is useful to distinguish pure and applied geometry. . . . *Pure geometry is a priori, but it is not synthetic . . . applied geometry is synthetic, but it is not a priori.* [Emphasis in original][8]

Salmon's empiricism shows in the first sentence above, that is, Wittgenstein's wall of separation is being appealed to. Pragmatists criticize Kant from a different angle.

Kant advanced epistemology about as far as possible while holding to the assumption that all statements were either analytic or synthetic. The latter were further subdivided into a priori and a posteriori. What is missing from this account is the idea of the function of statements. Is the statement, 'All swans are white' an analytic statement or a synthetic statement? For Kant, it had to be one or the other. But why could it not be analytic in one context and synthetic in another? There is nothing inherent in the syntax or semantics of the statement that determines which type of statement it is.

Piagetian Assimilation

A brief consideration of Piaget's notion of assimilation will help us further understand how Kant's argument can be put to work in educational psychology. Consider a cow eating grass and an owl seeking its prey. Cows can thrive on a certain range of plant tissue, while the owls cannot. What determines whether an animal can thrive on a given range of plants? This is not something cows and owls learn. The preestablished digestive structure determined by DNA calls the nutrition tune. Zoologists refer to the process of taking in food as assimilation. Piaget expanded this notion into cognitive development. If our DNA determines what can be assimilated as food or nourishment, then why doesn't it determine what we can assimilate in other ways? Our neurology takes the form it does because of the DNA code. We perceive the world by means of our eyes, retina, optic nerve, and so forth. This neurological equipment determines what we can perceive just as our gastric equipment determines what we can digest. This is no food-for-the-mind metaphor. Piaget argues that cognitive assimilation is just another dimension of biological assimilation. He is not using digestion as a model for learning. He is claiming that digestion and learning are instances of assimilation. To take just one more example: consider a bird that finds small pieces of plastic, which it uses to build a nest. Piaget says that the bird is assimilating new environmental elements into previously existing structures.

Piaget used the term 'development' and not 'learning', because his interest was less in the content of assimilation (what is assimilated) and more in how the structures that underlie assimilation develop. His conclusion is that the development of these structures is not quantitative (developing does not mean adding more), but qualitative. When our ability to assimilate, according to Piaget, improves, it does so categorically—not as a matter of degree. Such categorical changes were labeled "accommodation" by Piaget. Again, Piaget did not refer to his theory as a learning theory, because he views learning as assimilation. He saw himself as studying how cognitive structures develop, which he took to involve much more than learning processes.

While attention has been given to Piaget's views of development and what they might mean for classroom teachers, philosophy of education, with few exceptions, has not attempted to develop a view of education based on synthetic a priori epistemology.[9] It is surprising that the epistemological roots of Piaget have not received more attention from those who have embraced his thinking. I think that Piaget is seen by many in educational psychology as producing just another empirical theory that will stand or fall on the empirical evidence. My point is that it is a mistake to attempt to understand Piaget's ideas (and Dewey's) by means of an empiricist notion of a priori knowledge.

Finally, it is sometimes said that Piaget's theory of cognitive development is a further refinement of Dewey's ideas about the reconstruction of experience. This postulated relationship is further reinforced by Lawrence Kohlberg's comment that what he was doing was "Dewey warmed over." Kohlberg wanted to see his work as in the tradition of both Dewey and Piaget. As the investigation of the nature of the a priori reveals, a theory of moral development may not be consistent with both Dewey and Piaget. Kohlberg's writings constitute a significant part of the educational literature, but these writings are not in the epistemological tradition of pragmatism.[10]

The Pragmatic Conception of A Priori Knowledge

The empiricists' conception of the a priori is that which must be true in all possible worlds at all times. For this universal certitude they must give up content, for statements that are true in all possible worlds cannot inform us about this world. The rationalist conception of the a priori is a form that is inherent in the human mind-brain. We must be this kind of creature rather than that, and being this kind of creature means having certain innate capacities and limitations. These attributes form the content of our synthetic a priori knowledge, which is an expression of human nature. To gain this certitude, rationalists must open themselves to the possibility of having members of the list of synthetic a priori truths removed by subsequent research. How do we know what belongs on this list? We could simply solve all of the difficult problems by claiming they are on this list. For example, Kant sought to solve Hume's problem of induction by putting it on the synthetic a priori list.[11]

Both the analytic and synthetic conceptions of the a priori place scientific knowledge on a foundation of what can be known for sure, but what if we think of the a priori not as absolute but as contextual? If the a priori is *not* accepted as true in all possible worlds, as true come what may in experience, then it must be accepted in *some* contexts but not *all* contexts. This contextualization of the a priori will, of course, seem to some to be an argument for cultural or idiosyncratic relativism. The problem for pragmatism is to characterize a conception of the a priori that is neither (a) absolute across time and place, nor (b) culturally or personally relative.

Any inquiry must be launched from some intellectual platform. As C. S. Peirce points out, everything cannot be doubted at once. (I hear Descartes saying that someone must be doing the doubting, and that is not in doubt. But Peirce's point is organic, that is, anyone who believes *only* in her or his existence as a doubter is in serious cognitive and emotional difficulty.) As Dewey put it, "There is always something unquestioned in any problematic situation at any stage of its process." To this statement he attached the following footnote: "Of course, this very element may be the precarious, the ideal, and possibly the fanciful of some other situation. But it is to change the historic into the absolute to conclude that therefore everything is uncertain, all at once, or as such. This gives metaphysical skepticism as distinct from the working skepticism which is an inherent factor in all reflection and scientific inquiry."[12] Pragmatism rejects these absolutistic strategies and seeks a nonabsolutistic and nonrelativistic account of inquiry. How could we characterize such an intellectual platform?

Doubts must be expressed in some meaning system for them to be intelligible as doubts; we cannot doubt everything at once because there must be some meaning system that makes doubts intelligible but that cannot be part of the doubt itself. Inquiry must exist within some framework that allows it to make progress but that in turn places limitations on the conclusions of the inquiry.

The a priori in inquiry is a necessary instrument of thought that makes inquiry possible. We have seen two attempts to establish that which cannot be successfully doubted in any inquiry. These approaches assumed that the context of inquiry must be absolute. Pragmatists argue that what is undoubted in one context does not have to remain the undoubted in all other contexts. The undoubted in our investigations may itself come to be the focus of an investigation. This means that while pragmatists have to give up the certainty that comes with the absolutist strategy for characterizing the a priori of inquiry, they gain the ability to question or evaluate that which is assumed or taken for granted in their investigations. While some elements in every situation will have to be accepted, a priori, this is not to say that one may not change the context, and in that new context question these elements. However, in that new context, there will have to be some other givens—and so on it goes.

The doubted versus the undoubted distinction is always contextually contingent. What the epistemological naturalists argue is that attempts to set scientific inquiry upon an absolute or decontextualized base produces conceptions of the a priori that are too limited to support inquiry. As some philosophers of science would say, the absolute conceptions of the a priori have not been successful at showing us the rationality of scientific reasoning. Pragmatists will claim that the quest for certainty is self-defeating, and what is required is a nonabsolute conception of the a priori, a naturalizing of the a priori.

The framework for inquiry must be flexible enough to grow with the inquiry. This flexibility is achieved by interpreting the a priori as that which can be reconstructed in light of experience. Dewey used the expression "experimental logic" in this regard, though to empiricists this expression is an oxymoron. The pragmatic a priori is a systemic part of the knowledge for whose production it is an instrumentality.[13] The evaluation of this instrumentality is conducted in the history of ideas. The pragmatists of the Dewey era emphasized intellectual history of education because it is within this inquiry that we can determine how well the pragmatic a priori is serving inquiry. To evaluate methodological instrumentalities requires that the undoubted in one inquiry become the doubted in another inquiry.

The times when the meaning systems change Kuhn referred to as scientific revolutions. When scientists are following the established rules, the area of scientific inquiry is in a period of normal science. When the a priori of the science changes, the revolution occurs, and the period of extraordinary science is produced. Why do such changes occur? When some of the researchers can make a convincing case for modifying the a priori guiding the inquiry, more and more participants begin to move toward the new paradigm. As the a priori is recognized as playing a more relaxed role in science, one expects that it will become the object of thought by more and more scientists.

How should one expect to modify the inquiry-guiding a priori? While the expression "naturalizing the a priori" is open to many interpretations, what Dewey and the other pragmatists were up to can be seen in the *principle of continuity.*[14] As we modify the framework or paradigm of inquiry, we should not attempt to create new paradigms that break the continuity with the present frameworks. New forms emerge from what exists. One cannot break completely with the present and start over entirely. (David Denby presents an interesting discussion of this point within the context of traditional literature.)[15]

The a priori in our inquiry provides the frame of reference—something to hold on to come what may in *this* experience. We require an a priori to observe the world, that is, to have experience; this was Kant's point to Hume. The empiricist's view of the a priori is as a set of logical rules for processing data that was generated or collected *independently.* Kant's argument is that the a priori actually served in the collection of evidence; evidence is evidence because of the a priori. Kant's conception of the a priori, however, is something fixed prior to experience.

Kant analyzed propositions as being either analytic or synthetic. Holding to this method of statement analysis, Kant took logic about as far as possible, without the introduction of another dimension of language. This additional element has typically been referred to by pragmatists as 'function'. If one reads the sentence, 'All Swans are white', part of the meaning of this statement is involved in determining whether this is an analytic or synthetic statement. That is, can we have black swans? If we cannot, by definition, then we know the statement 'All swans are white' is functioning analytically. If there can be black swans whose existence would prove the statement 'All swans are white' false, then the statement 'All swans are white' is functioning synthetically.

If we hear someone say, 'All swans are white', we can legitimately wonder if this statement is functioning analytically or synthetically for the speaker. Within Kantian epistemology, the statement, not the speaker, bears the attributes analytic or synthetic. John Austin's distinction between *illocutionary force* and *perlocutionary force* is helpful in this regard.[16] A locution is a speech act, such as 'All swans are white'. The perlocutionary force of this statement is the actual empirical effect that the speaker's speech act has on the hearer. Perlocutionary force derives from what the speaker does *by* saying something. Illocutionary force stems from what the speaker does *in* saying something.

We can now see that when someone says, 'All swans are white', and means that a black swan-appearing bird cannot be a swan, then the illocutionary force of the speech act is analytic, or a priori in the empiricists' sense. If the person means that we can look but we will never find a nonwhite swan, then the statement has synthetic illocutionary force. Now consider Dewey's remark, "Any conclusion reached by an inquiry that is taken to warrant the conclusion is 'final' *for that case.* 'Final' here has logical force."[17] The logical force of which he wrote is something very like the illocutionary force discussed by John Austin. Dewey is very clearly pointing to a contextualized illocutionary force. What could this mean? I submit that Dewey was pointing us to the pragmatic a priori, but without the benefit of Austin's important distinction. The empiricists' sense of 'analytic' can be defined as that which cannot be consistently denied. For the pragmatists, we will have to modify this to mean that which cannot be consistently denied in this problematic context. What is analytic in one context may not be (contra Kant) in another. In other words, the illocutionary force of statements may change from one context to another. It is in this sense that Dewey naturalized the a priori of inquiry.

The philosophic question is 'to which statements do we grant the attribute undoubtedness?' Which statements do we consider having a priori force? Methodologically, how do we know what not to doubt at any given time? What is required is a new methodological conception of philosophic analysis. More accurately, what is required is a methodology for explicating the pragmatic a priori, because this notion is essential to establishing a naturalized view of conceptual analysis.

The meaning of terms or the nature of concepts has its roots in human experience, and conceptual analysts must be as comprehensive as possible in their consideration of it. Naturalized conceptual analysis must reach into the past for meaning and must consider the best scientific work at hand as well. How do we extract meaning from the past? The fall of logical empiricism makes this question very important. What normative principles regulate this reaching into the past for conceptual meaning? Having rejected analyticity and theory-free observation, how do we prevent the use of the history of ideas from becoming political revisionism?

Before saying more about the nature of this task, we must consider the justification issue. In other words, there is a distinction between characterizing scientific inference or explanation and justifying scientific inference or explanation. I have alluded to the characterization problem for a naturalized conception of conceptual analysis, but before pursuing that problem further, we should consider the justification problem. Of course, I cannot justify a methodology before it has been characterized, but we can explore the possible ways that pragmatic philosophy has dealt with justification issues as a kind of advance organizer for what is to be attempted.

Pragmatism and the Circular-Reasoning Issue

In several earlier papers, I have tried to argue that we could include scientific findings in philosophic analysis without giving up the legitimacy of the methodology.[18] I thought that by attending to the goals of inquiry, what were in those days often referred to as epistemic utilities, we could avoid the absolutism of First Philosophy's reliance on analyticity while at the same time not falling into cultural relativism. Steven Stich has more recently addressed this point.

> The charge that I heard most often was that relativistic accounts of cognitive assessment play into the hands of epistemic nihilists because they abandon any serious attempt to separate good cognitive strategies from bad ones. For both the relativists and the nihilist, it was said, "anything goes." But this . . . is just a mistake as far as epistemic pragmatism is concerned. The pragmatic assessment of cognitive strategies is certainly relativistic, but it is no more nihilistic than the pragmatic assessment of investment strategies or engineering techniques.[19]

Moreover, Stich addresses what he sees as the question of circular reasoning: it may be objected, "that pragmatism is viciously circular, since there is no way we could show that our cognitive system is pragmatically preferable without using the very system whose superiority we are trying to establish."[20] Recall Hume's argument that inductive inference cannot be justified inductively under pain of circular reasoning. Stich is raising Hume's objection for the pragmatic view of a priori knowledge.

Giere claims, as noted in the previous chapter, that philosophy of science is itself a science,[21] but he rejects the complete social constructivist view of scientific concepts. The conclusion that social reality is a social construction "by itself, provides no evidence that *natural* reality is similarly constructed."[22] As he sees it, "There is indeed something important missing from the sociological account. That something is not rationality, but causal interaction between scientists and the world."[23] In place of methodological foundationism, he looks toward studies of "various biologically based cognitive capacities including perception, motor control, memory, imagination, and language." Moreover, "a cognitive theory of science would attempt to explain how scientists use these capacities for interacting with the world as they go about the business of constructing modern science."[24]

Why do creatures such as ourselves learn to extract meaning from and develop theories about the world in the ways that we do? These are inchoate, but clear, problems that form a basis for studying how we think about our experience. Giere must surely be correct in claiming that the application of the results of cognitive-scientific studies to the study of scientific methodology is essential in this endeavor. It is difficult to see how learning more about our cognitive processes would not help us be better scientists and philosophers. The task that Giere has cut out for himself is to show us how cognitive science, whose results are directly relevant to explaining why scientists do what they do, can be used in the study of science without allowing his methodology to simply turn back on itself and thereby encounter the circular-reasoning objection. Clearly normative methodological questions about the proper conduct of cognitive science cannot be answered by simply doing cognitive science. What we require is an elaboration of how normative discourse serves within cognitive science. (Note that there emerges from Giere's approach an unpredicted interface between philosophy of education and philosophy of science; answers to the question 'What is learning?' become central to both philosophic efforts.)

Giere is clear that the adequacy of his view of philosophy of science as a science turns on the circular reasoning issue—what he calls *reflexivity*. Consider his statement: "Developing a scientific theory is a reflexive enterprise in the sense that one is practicing a form of the very kind of activity under study. Thus, one necessarily begins with some commitments about one's subject embedded in one's own practice. This need not lead to paradox or irredeemable bias so long as one is able to change one's practices in the light of one's own findings. But because the mechanisms of self-correction may be fairly inefficient, it is important that one begin with a good first approximation."[25] I submit that this statement is compatible with the pragmatic conception of the a priori and that its further development would provide a solution to the circle problem with which Giere is concerned.

There is one important caution, however. To "change one's practices in the light of one's own findings" is what we mean by 'learning'; but, when we are thinking about the role of a priori knowledge in inquiry, simply changing one's practices in light of findings can be *ad hoc*ery. If I can modify my assumptions in light of data, I can make any set of data support to a lesser or greater degree some tenaciously held conclusion. (This is a form of the objection raised against the Bayesian inference approach to scientific justification—can you change your prior probabilities when the data begin to roll in?) The pragmatic conception of the a priori knowledge that guides an inquiry must be *independent* of the conclusions of the inquiry that it supports. It is by no means obvious how we can do this. How do we explicate (identify and justify) the a priori dimension of inquiry in light of actual scientific conclusions, then use this content in the conduct of subsequent inquiry, and not be open to the charge of circular reasoning? This is Giere's question put in pragmatic terms.

Stich fends off the circular-reasoning objection with an argument that goes as follows: making an evaluation of the adequacy of an epistemological thesis about the nature of cognition is a cognitive process. "So according to the critic, what we should want is an account of cognitive evaluation that can be applied without any cognitive activity at all. Surely, at this juncture, the right reply to make is that this is a perfectly preposterous thing to want. The 'defect' that the critic has discovered in the pragmatic account (and all others) is simply that we can't apply it without thinking."[26] How could we ever know about our cognitive processes if we do not use our cognitive processes? To understand thinking, we have to think about it. (Dewey once observed that philosophy emerged when thinking became conscious of itself.) We know that the claim, 'X may not be used to study X' is false. But if you are thinking that this seems to interpret the circle problem in the most benign way, you are right. Stich is missing Giere's point that while we can obviously use cognitive science to study how scientists think, the circularity problem enters as a *normative* problem. How can we use cognitive science to warrant the methods of science? This is Giere's *reflexivity* problem. In other words, while it is obvious that we can use cognitive science to study science, we have not addressed Hume's objection, which is that there is no scientific justification for being scientific.

Metamethodology

As part of the growing number of malcontents with methodological foundationism, the metamethodologists (a term coined by Lakatos) set out to examine the various characterizations of scientific methodology and then to investigate which of these methodologies is the most effective in solving scientific problems. To assess the problem-solving effectiveness of the various methodologies requires a methodology. What would this methodology be? The approach of the metamethodologists is to create a hierarchical conception of scientific methodology in which scientific research is conducted at level one and evaluated at level two, the metamethodological level. It is at the second level that disagreements about various first-level methodologies are investigated and resolved by measuring their problem-solving effectiveness.[27] In this way, it is argued, we will have a measure of a given research program's progress and, hence, of its rationality.

Laudan considered this approach wrongheaded:

> The metamethodology associated with Kuhn, Feyerabend, and Lakatos . . . applies the methodology under review to prominent historical cases, e.g., the choice between Cartesian or Newtonian physics, or between Newtonian and relativistic physics. In each case, one asks which rival the methodology would have picked out, assuming that it had available all and only the evidence which was accessible to the content parties. One then compares the theory choices mandated by the methodology with the theory choices made by consensus of the great scientists who brought the episode to a close. If the methodology leads to choices congruent with those actually made by the scientific elite, then—according to the historicists—it has exhibited the rationality of those choices and the scientists who made them, and has established its own credentials.[28]

If the methodology being evaluated points us to choices at odds with those of the elite, then the methodology should be rejected.

The metamethodological program always struck me as strange, in light of Carnap's failure with his inductive logic. Carnap set out to interpret inductive inference as partial entailment. Actually this is a wonderful idea that someone would eventually have to explore; fortunately for us, Carnap did it early on. In deductive arguments, the content of the conclusions cannot exceed the content of the premises. Inductive arguments are ampliative in that they produce conclusions whose content does exceed the content of the premises. Carnap set out to study what we might call the degree of amplification. The difficulty he encountered is the selection of a measure function. How do we measure the degree of entailment involved in a given inductive argument? It turns out that there is no nonarbitrary way to select this measure function. This matter is lucidly discussed by Salmon.[29]

One might quite legitimately wonder whether metamethodology leads to an infinite regress; what about creating a third level of methodology, the metametamethodological level, to assess the effectiveness of metamethodology?

Laudan rejects this much hierarchy in our conception of "scientific debates" in favor of what he calls a "reticulated model" of scientific rationality. He does not think that three levels are required to carry on debates about the best approach to scientific rationality. His approach to avoiding the third level is to validate metamethodology in terms of the goals of first level methodology. As he states, "we can use our knowledge of the available methods of inquiry as a tool for assessing the viability of proposed cognitive aims."[30]

Giere's criticism of the metamethodological approach is its grounding in our intuitions about science. "This is a rather weak foundation. And like an explication, it provides no protection from relativism. The logic is at best *descriptive* of *our* intuitions. It does not insure us that our intuitions themselves are correct."[31] How good are our intuitions about how science should be done and what it should produce? (We run into the folk psychology problem once again.) Thus, the explication of intuitions cannot avoid the charge of arbitrariness. As Giere further argues, while metamethodology set out to construct a normative conception of science, it was unable to generate anything we could think of as having *normative* force. As Giere complains,

> Does the type of metamethodology advocated by Lakatos and Laudan yield methodological principles which are genuinely normative? Not really. . . . metamethodology would tell us only that we had discovered *descriptions* of situations which we intuitively regard as clear cases of rational acceptance or pursuit. We might have correctly identified the descriptive component of the methodology, without capturing its normative force. To claim we had captured the normative component would require that we make the judgments we do *because* of considerations based on problem-solving effectiveness. In Kantian terms, Laudan's metamethodology could at most show only that we are acting in accord with his methodology, not that we are acting out of regard for that methodology. It cannot show that his methodology is actually embodied as a norm in our judgments. [Emphasis in original][32]

For any account of methodology to be adequate, it must have normative force. It is not enough to show that one's view of methodology describes what is being done because this would not show, as Giere puts it, a "regard for that methodology." The methodology of conceptual analysis I am advocating here runs no risk of simply describing what is being done because no one, as far as I can tell, is even trying to do that. My problem is to create a *regard for* this methodology, which is to show its normative value.

Giere also objects that the metamethodologists do not deal directly with the problem of circularity. As he observes,

The connection between metamethodology and the circle argument is as follows. If Lakatos and Laudan really had been taking a naturalistic approach to methodology, they would have adopted the reflexive strategy of applying their methodology to itself. This, however, is not their official doctrine. That they deliberately avoided a reflexive strategy *because* of its obvious circularity, I cannot say. Their metamethodologies, however, are not reflexive and thus not blatantly circular. Whether they can achieve their ends while still avoiding circularity is another question.[33]

Giere's point is that if philosophy of science is itself a science, as some epistemological naturalists claim, then the reflexivity or circularity problem must be dealt with. Not only has Laudan addressed the circularity problem (perhaps he had not by the publication date of Giere's book), but he has done so in a fashion that advances instrumentalism.

Inchoate Versus Developed Instrumentalism

In its simplest form, 'instrumentalism' refers to the view that some action or principle is justified if it can be shown to achieve (cause, produce, bring about, effect) some desirable outcome. Instrumentalists consider claims about effects or consequences as typical assertions of the type common to science, that is, assertions evaluated as scientific claims—by means of scientific methodology. So, inchoate instrumentalism assumes that we know which possible ends are desirable and that we have at hand a legitimate scientific methodology to assess effectiveness claims.

The typical philosopher of education is now focused on the question: How do we know the projected or actual outcome is desirable? As we will see, some argue that instrumentalism is unable to justify ends or goals and is useful only as a device for legitimating means. I promise to focus on this question in chapter 6, but for now let's consider the question of scientific methodology. If you think instrumentalism will have a difficult time convincing you that it can legitimate ends or goals, note that the problem of legitimating scientific methodology is no less awesome.

Let's make scientific methodology the *evaluandum* (that which is being evaluated). An instrumental evaluation requires a specification of desirable ends that this methodology has to achieve to receive a positive evaluation. And now we are faced with the goals-of-science question. But again, we have another problem to solve. Arbitrarily select any goal-candidate for the goal-of-science position. How do we know that the methodology being evaluated can achieve that goal? The answer cannot be "by typical scientific methodology," because it is that very methodology that is being evaluated. Recall Hume's circularity argument. Are the instrumentalists shown to be out of steam at this point?

Naturalists, such as Laudan, accept the challenge, that is, they claim that to naturalize philosophy of science requires a means-ends analysis of scientific methodology. As Laudan puts it, "I submit that *all* methodological rules (at least all of those rules and constraints of the sort usually debated among methodologists) can be recast as contingent statements . . . about connections between ends and means" (emphasis in original).[34] He then notes that when we set out to justify a methodological rule, we have to appeal to methodological rules. "How," he asks, "do we either break the circle or block the regress?" His solution is to "find some warranting or evidencing principle which all the disputing theories of methodology share in common. If such a principle— accepted by all of the contending parties—exists, then it can be invoked as a neutral and impartial vehicle for choosing between rival methodologies." But Laudan wonders whether we have any reason "to believe that all of the major theories of scientific methodology . . . share certain principles of empirical support, which can be treated as 'noncontroversial' for purposes of choosing between them." He formulates a rudimentary rule that captures "our normal inductive convictions." "If actions of a particular sort, m, have consistently promoted certain cognitive ends, e, in the past, and rival actions, n, have failed to do so, then assume that future actions following the rule 'if your aim is e, you ought to do m' are more likely to promote those ends than actions based on the rule 'if your aim is e, you ought to do n.' " This rule "appears to be a sound rule for learning from experience," and if it is not, then "no general rule is."[35]

Furthermore, Laudan claims that this rule is "arguably assumed universally among philosophers of science," including the historical school therein—"their entire program rests on the assumption that we can learn something from the past about how scientific rationality works." Without this rule, or one very close to it, Laudan claims, the historical approach would be unable to critique logical positivism—which is thought by many to be its claim to fame. Laudan goes on to build upon his rudimentary rule as a metamethodological device for selecting among the various theories of methodology—discussions of which constitute most of the twentieth-century literature in philosophy of science.

Laudan claims that his rule captures what is undoubted in the methodological problem-solving situation. He is using the undoubted within the problem context to generate a solution. Giere is going to claim that Laudan's methodological rule is, nevertheless, descriptive, and the *fact* that this rule is undoubted in the context of methodological theory does not give the rule normative force. The idea of appealing to what is undoubted in a problem situation is clearly appealing to a factual (descriptive) attribute of the situation. Whatever analytical methodology we use to establish the undoubted, we are attempting to establish a matter of fact. Within this or that context with these or those principles established as undoubted, certain actions are warranted while other actions are not.

This takes us into the teeth of the central problem for naturalized epistemology. We must embrace C. S. Peirce's distinction between (a) "living doubt" ("Living doubt is the life of investigation") and (b) "idle make-believe" doubt (what we might refer to as 'hypothetical doubt').[36] In an actual problem-solving context, we find people with hopes and fears trying to achieve certain objectives while trying to avoid certain pitfalls. Problem solving takes place within a highly cognitive and valuational situation where there are both areas of living doubt and areas of living certitude. The living doubt fires the inquiry, while the living certitude gives inquiry a context in which to develop. Laudan's point is that some aspects of scientific methodology are not being doubted. But can't skilled rhetoricians (and, of course, lawyers) create doubt where there was none before? (Apparently any run-of-the-mill salesperson can remove doubt.) It is well-known that philosophers can find interesting and sometimes compelling ways to raise doubts. How can naturalism deal with hypothetical doubt?

A real problem-solving situation is characterized by (a) the initial conditions, values, and relationships that are undoubted and (b) the problem that is being questioned or investigated. If the undoubted is questioned to the extent that at some point so much doubt is created about that which was originally accepted, then that original problem-solving context is pushed aside in favor of a new problematic context. The naturalists do not take themselves to be thinking about formal logic or analyticity; rather, they are concerned with what people actually doubt and do not doubt. Beginning to hypothesize doubts is to leave the situation or context intellectually and to attempt to create another. This may be an effective political ploy: keep challenging assumptions as a way to prevent the originating doubts from receiving analysis. (I recall one well-known philosopher of education saying that when a committee is pursuing synthesis, emphasize analysis; and when the committee is engaging in analysis, stress the value of synthesis.)

Every problem-solving context is dynamic in that conditions are rarely stable over long periods, at least where thinking is going on. Moreover, the distinction between the doubted and the undoubted is never going to be mathematically precise. Yearning for a decontextualized rule for separating the two is an urge to rebuild Wittgenstein's wall. (It is possible that skilled rhetoricians or negotiators could produce agreement, that is, undoubtedness, from considerable real and living doubt. Should these rhetoricians and negotiators be seeking to remove doubt? This is a normative question that changes the context of inquiry.)

A developed instrumentalism will have to deal with the question of ends or goals. As Laudan makes clear, the "aims of science vary and quite appropriately so from one epoch to another, from one scientific field to another, and sometimes among researchers in the same field."[37] Laudan's discussion of the goals or ends of scientific inquiry clearly points us in the direction of pragmatism and Dewey's theory of instrumental logic, including its thesis about the justification of ends. Contemporary naturalists are aware that Dewey's arguments are related to their efforts. For example, Philip Kitcher comments in a footnote that he will "not try to trace the ways in which ideas of Peirce and Dewey are recast in the writings of contemporary epistemologists."[38] Laudan remarked, "Scientific methodology is itself a scientific discipline which cannot dispense with the very methods of inquiry whose validity it investigates. . . . More than half a century ago, John Dewey—ever eager to naturalize the a priori—repudiated that conception of methodology which saw it as 'an affair . . . of fixed first principles . . . of methodology which Neo-scholastics called criteriology.' "[39] Laudan's instrumental arguments about the justification of scientific methodology are similar to, if not contiguous with, Dewey's approach to logic and the a priori.

Explicating the Pragmatic A Priori

The Context of Meaning

Having rejected decontextualized knowledge, we know that what we assume about the universe in our studies of it will be materially linked with the conclusions of these studies. The late Philip G. Smith used to say that "circular reasoning was not bad so long as we use really large circles." People saw this comment to be as much humor as epistemology, but I believe his point is that we must attempt to create a large gap between the a priori we use to structure the problem that will guide the inquiry at hand and the set of possible solutions to this problem. Having given up the certainty provided by the analytic a priori, we must admit that we can make mistakes and at times draw conclusions that are more circular than we realize. We cannot see the future, and we will frequently find that the best solution is not in the set of possible solutions (alternative hypotheses) we envisioned at the outset of inquiry. The conclusion drawn might turn out in subsequent analyses to be more dependent on the undoubted than the data generated by the doubted. Moreover, the more people who are engaged in an inquiry, the better the chances of such small circles being detected. As inquiry progresses, the size of the circle of reasoning will grow; that is, as we learn more and more about the universe, the larger the content of the pragmatic a priori and the larger the scope of the undoubted.

The pragmatic conception of a priori knowledge is that which is taken as the undoubted framework of a particular context of problem solving. When empiricists engaged in conceptual analysis, they were attempting to establish the meaning of terms that would subsequently be used in some type of problem-solving. They viewed their analyses as *prior* to the substantive decision-making that would follow. In the view of naturalists, the empiricists were trying to establish the meaning context of inquiry, a problem that both schools of thought agree must be solved.

To make the role of pragmatic a priori knowledge in an inquiry more than a logical possibility, a methodology for its enucleation from human experience must be characterized and justified. In keeping with the plan of this book, we will investigate the role of a naturalized view of conceptual analysis as a way of explicating part of the a priori knowledge related to a given area of inquiry. There are two dimensions of this explication process that should be separated as we pursue this methodology.

First, a dimension of the context of inquiry related to the establishment of the meaning of terms is historical-intellectual meaning, which is to be found by investigating our semantic endowment. At this stage in the development of philosophy of education there exists a rich history of ideas that was generated over two and a half millennia. The perspective for our current efforts that this historical-intellectual activity affords us should not be overlooked. Within the history of ideas, there are philosophic and scientific arguments that can contribute meaning to our analyses. (Earlier versions of conceptual analysis often mentioned the origin of terms, but discussions of the role these terms played in previous inquiry was often elided.)

Second, part of the cognitive context of any instance of problem-solving is the current technical or scientific meaning of terms. Such meanings may be largely implicit, that is, terms come into use having never been explicitly defined. After the fashion of Kuhnian incommensurability, one term may mean different things to different theories or paradigms.

How does the current scientific meaning relate to the historical-intellectual meaning? One may exist without the other. If an area of scientific research is producing discourse about various relationships, terms may be used that were either generated within this research or modified for it. But if an area of educational interest is not receiving scientific attention, then the historical-intellectual meaning may be the only material for analysis. More commonly, there is both historical-intellectual meaning and current scientific theoretical-meaning, and the two are not well-articulated because there are two discrete sets of language users. If we are to establish background meaning in this kind of situation, conceptual analysis will have to bring both sources of meaning together to form a view of the concept in question that is both true to the central aspects of the historical-intellectual meaning and can at the same time provide direction for subsequent scientific inquiry. Conceptual analysis is constructive in this sense. It is also normative in that its results are claimed to be the best account of the concept, that is, the meaning that *should* be attributed to the term.

Note that to select the appropriate technical meaning of a term may involve us directly in the problem of induction, sometimes referred to as the problem of 'theory acceptance'. The meaning of technical terms derives from the theoretical context in which they are serving, and if there are theoretical issues involved in what a term means, the adequate specification of meaning of a technical term will involve a kind of *meaning acceptance* on the part of the analysts. Stated differently, conclusions about the meaning of terms in a given literature—and this is true of ordinary language analysis as well—are inductive conclusions in that they are contingent results of inquiry. These conclusions are also normative in the sense that they rest on analyses of conditions and consequences of use and are submitted as having normative force. We will explore this point further in the following chapter.

A Recent Example

An example of the kind of conceptual analysis I have been describing is provided by Jerome Kagan in his book *Galen's Prophecy*,[40] where he attempts to develop an analysis of 'temperament' as a conceptual origin for the development of a theory of temperament. Note that I am not making a judgment about the adequacy of Kagan's research and conclusions about the nature of child temperament; what I am saying is that he offers us a case of conceptual analysis that (a) is clearly intended to give direction to further scientific research and

(b) is not an instance of empiricistic analysis. Kagan is, of course, concerned with the current findings in psychology and neuroscience, but he also conducts an analysis of the concept of temperament by looking into the deep past. In place of topological matrices built of stipulative definitions, he considers a wide range of historical uses of the concept of temperament. I cite Kagan's work as constituting some evidence for the claim that there are examples of conceptual analysis that are based on a naturalized view of a priori knowledge. The further development of the methodology for extracting conceptual meaning from human intellectual experience remains as a most important task before us.

Central to Kagan's research is a distinction between inhibited children and uninhibited children. What distinction could be more straightforward? Create two categories, give them some kind of operational rules, and collect data. But Kagan never produces such a topology. He begins, instead, with a historical analysis of the area of inquiry. Galen, a second-century physician, was concerned with the concept of temperament, which he separated into nine types based on four humors. These temperaments are as follows:

1. Ideal personality balance
2. Cold
3. Dry
4. Hot
5. Moist
6. Melancholic
7. Choleric
8. Sanguine
9. Phlegmatic

These ideas were used by Hippocrates (born 460 B.C.) to explain the relationship between racial and climatic differences. Galen's ideas remained viable in North Africa and the Middle East until the nineteenth century. Kagan reports that in 1861 Alexander Bain argued that there are biological differences among people that explain differences among ethnic groups. Long before Galen, the Chinese were investigating temperament differences and drawing conclusions that were in many ways similar to his. It was Freud who began to separate phobias and depression. As Kagan notes, "For two thousand years the melancholic profile consisted of a blend of depression and fear, with the former given slightly greater emphasis than the latter. Perhaps the real but modest association between anxiety and depression made it easy for most observers to assume that the correlation was greater than it actually was." If we had not already suspected it, the concept of temperament is (a) integrally involved with many other concepts, and (b) paradigmatic; as Kagan speculates, "Perhaps one reason why the ancients did not distinguish between fear and depression was that doing so would have created a need for a fifth personality type and marred the perfect symmetry of a system that had one major personality type for each pair of qualities."[41]

Principles of Pragmatic Analysis

From the considerations of this chapter, several aspects of what a reconstructed notion of conceptual analysis might be begin to appear. To conduct a historical analysis of the term 'temperament' involves examining all past scholarship that was concerned with the concept, while asking ourselves:

(a) What was the rationale or justification for these studies? Why was this concept being studied? What use was made of the results of these studies?

(b) What alternative definitions or meanings were rejected and why? What conceptual issues or tensions existed and why did the scholars make the meaning decisions they did?

(c) How was the term in question related to other terms?

The historical analysis of a concept will be especially concerned with abrupt changes or turns in development because these developmental changes could well indicate issues that have contemporary significance for our definitions or hypotheses. As noted, Freud was the first theorist to distinguish phobias and depression. We would want to know what led him to make this distinction as well as its consequences for temperament theory.

Note that this is a normative process. Some instances of scholarship will be rejected on grounds of low utility, that is, nothing significant was achieved semantically or evidentially. Any review of the past will be selective. If inquiry were a one-person operation, such selection could well lead to a biased account of the history of scholarship in question, but given that many different scholars will make and review these judgments and hold various conversations about them, 'making judgments' can be thought of as something done by a community of inquirers. And if a few divergent thinkers disagree with the judgment of the scholarly community, they are free to go their own way and to develop their theses. Understanding is often improved through juxtaposition.

While the history of ideas is a primary source of a priori knowledge, parallel inquiries are also important. Kagan makes a typical naturalist point:

> The environmental explanation of why a child was excessively fearful was so familiar and reasonable that most psychologists were reluctant to relinquish it until another, equally commanding one was provided. Neuroscientists were supplying these new explanations with fresh facts and arguments that assumed inherited variation in neurochemistry and neurophysiology. Alvin Weinberg, a former director of the Oak Ridge Laboratory in Tennessee, has noted that any scientific domain that illuminates a neighboring one has proved to be of great value in science. Study of temperament requires the understanding of behavior, affect, and physiology; hence, it should contribute to each of these related fields of scholarship.[42]

There is, to some degree, a kind of intellectual reciprocity among inquiries where the benefits often move back and forth among various studies. (I can imagine Dewey pointing us to his principle of the continuity of knowledge and growth. This reciprocity—or continuity—is often obscured by the rigidity of university curriculum categories as presented to students in course catalogs, school or departmental organizational structures, and faculty turf-minding behavior.)

This methodology of explicating a priori knowledge is a central goal for traditional naturalistic epistemology. A problematic situation must exist so that its warranted solution has value for theorists or practitioners. In light of this problematic situation, an investigation of prior inquiries is conducted, using the methods adumbrated above. As Putnam states in his recent book on pragmatism, Dewey recognized that we can never make the methods of inquiry into algorithms, and we can never find a "metaphysical guarantee" that we have found some precious set of foundational beliefs that will never require revision. But this, "does not mean that we don't know *anything* about how to conduct inquiry. Pierce and Dewey believed that we *have* learned a good deal about how inquiry should be conducted—learned from our past experience with inquiry—and that some of what we have learned applies to inquiry in general, and not just to particular kinds of inquiry or particular subject matters" (emphasis in original).[43]

5

THE STRUCTURE OF CONCEPTS

Introduction

It was argued in the previous chapter that the distinction between analytic and contextualized a priori knowledge allows for the reconstruction of the methodology of conceptual analysis, the goals of which are the explication of pragmatic a priori knowledge that exists with human experience. While conceptual analysis draws from the history of ideas, understanding how people form concepts is also relevant. In this chapter I attempt to show that a naturalistic notion of conceptual analysis is further supported by recent philosophic thought on the nature of conceptual structures and conceptual learning.

Philosophy of education during the analytic period made use of methodologies of conceptual analysis, but, because of its belief in a wall of separation between philosophy and psychology, it never addressed the relationship between the concept meaning enucleated by its methodology and the nature of conceptual learning. If, however, we lower the wall between philosophy and psychology, as both the epistemological naturalists and cognitive scientists are attempting to do, we can ask about the nature of conceptual learning, and how what we know about this learning might relate to our understanding of the methodology of conceptual analysis.

What Are Concepts?

It is useful to think about concepts as a quadratic relationship among names, definitions, referents (sometimes called denotations), and contexts of use. (See figure 1.) Within a given context, conceptual meaning is constructed from the triadic relationship of words, what they name, and their definitions. The name of the concept names the members of the referent set, sometimes known in logic as the *extension* of a term. A definition establishes a relationship between a word defined and a set of defining characteristics of that word, sometimes known in logic as the *intension* (rather than intention) of a term. This means

Context

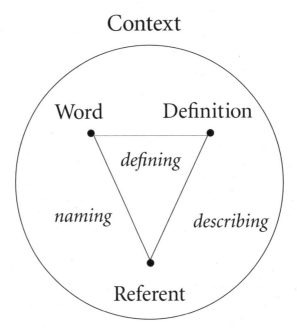

Fig. 1. The quadratic nature of concepts

that the defining conditions presented in the definition constitute a description of the members of the reference set, which is a relationship too often ignored in discourses on "conceptual learning" and "how to teach concepts." When the word is 'sloop', the definition is: a sailboat with one mast, two sails, and a single jib (the front sail). The characteristics listed in the definition *define* the word 'sloop' and *describe* the essential (defining) features of sloops.

Figure 2 indicates that there are also six basic logical forms that conceptual questions may assume, an observation important for testmakers. These forms are exemplified as follows:

1. A sailboat with one mast, two sails, and a single jib defines what word?
2. What is the definition of 'sloop'?
3. What does 'sloop' name?
4. What is the name of this boat?
5. Point out a boat with one mast, two sails, and a single jib.
6. Describe this boat.

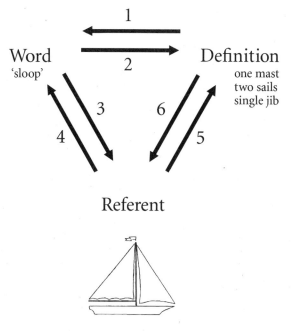

Fig. 2. The concept of 'sloop'

Students who have, as we say, the concept of sloop can answer each of these question with equal facility.

Open Versus Closed Definitions

Methodological foundationism sought to reconstruct scientific knowledge in terms of logicomathematical structure, an approach that greatly influenced how scientific theories were interpreted. Part of this formalistic view of science included formal structures for constructing definitions. Some definitions, such as those for the words 'sloop' and 'triangle', can be stated in terms of conditions that are individually necessary and jointly sufficient, which means that each condition is necessary or indispensable to the definition. Together the various necessary conditions are sufficient for a unique identification of the extension (the referent set) of the term. These definitions could reasonably be referred to as *closed* definitions because the extension of the term defined is unambiguously established. In other words, the defining conditions specify precise inclusion and exclusion criteria for the referent of the term defined. What I am calling closed definitions were considered, by those who sought to reconstruct science as a formal structure, to be the standard in light of which all technical definitions should be created.

The goal of analytic philosophy of education was to establish and evaluate the meaning of terms that were prominent in educational discourse. Behind the scenes in such analyses there was the "individually necessary and jointly sufficient conditions" notion of conceptual adequacy. Analytic philosophy could not be expected to complete definitions for concepts that were vague or unfinished; the best that one could expect in such situations was a partial definition. Analyses of the terms 'teaching', 'explaining', and 'understanding' are such examples. Not being able to state necessary and sufficient conditions, we could, nevertheless, state some of the conditions, which would help clarify some of what was at issue.

Peter Achinstein argues that for some important scientific words we cannot specify necessary and sufficient conditions.

> Among the properties of metals frequently cited are hardness, high conductivity, high melting point, metallic luster, solid at room temperature, ductility, malleability, and opacity. Yet mercury, a metal, is liquid at room temperature, and the alkali metals (lithium, sodium, and so on) are soft and have low melting points. Dictionaries will often employ terms like "most," "generally," and "typically," when listing properties possessed by many, though not all, types of items to which the term is actually applied.[1]

This suggests that for terms such as 'metal', the best we can do is to state conditions that cluster around the concept. These definitions could be called *open* definitions, and be said to underpin open concepts.

These open-textured definitions will be judged as inferior to closed definitions by those who embrace a logicomathematical model for conceptual meaning. Since the reemergence of naturalized epistemology, especially its view that there is no sharp distinction between philosophy and psychology, open definitions are held up as not only acceptable but as explanatory of the structure of scientific theories.[2]

Graded Conceptual-Structures

The defining characteristics of what I am calling open concepts (definitions that do not form a set of necessary and sufficient conditions for extension of the concept) have important consequences for how we think about both the *extension* (the set of instances) and the *intension* (set of defining conditions) of the concept. Note that student conceptual learning occurs both in terms of the extension and intension. While it is not recognized as such by young students, constructing and reconstructing conceptual meanings is the intellectual manipulation and experimentation of the interaction between extensions and intensions. A penetrating analysis of conceptual learning requires that we attend to the notion of conceptual grading.

Extensional Gradings

Some researchers have conducted "free response experiments" in which subjects are asked to list examples of a category with which they are presented.[3] For example, subjects are given the category name, 'bird', and asked to provide instances of that category. One set of outcomes is as follows:

ROBIN	377
EAGLE	161
WREN	83
CHICKEN	40
OSTRICH	17
BAT	3

In this case, 'robin' was the most frequently selected member of the extension of the concept 'bird'. This is taken as evidence for the thesis that some members of the extension are more central to the concept than are other members. In other words, the members of the extension of 'bird' came be graded in terms of the centrality to the meaning of the term. Other studies support this notion: subjects are asked to judge the truth of sentences as they appear on a computer screen, such as "A duck is a bird" or "A robin is a fruit." Reaction times were faster and the number of errors lower for sentences that used the basic or central instances of a concept than for sentences that used peripheral instances.[4]

When I ask my students to give an instance of the category 'bird', 95 percent of them will list 'cardinal'. This gives us a wonderful example of how cultural diversity participates in our concepts. I do not know if it is because of the geographical location of the university and student body, the Saint Louis baseball team, or some peculiarity in the study cited above, but the fact that no one listed cardinal in that study while virtually all of my students do shows us, in a fairly concrete case, that we should pay attention to sociocultural and ethnic differences. These kinds of considerations show us that the extensions of many terms are graded, in the sense that their instantiations range from basic (central) to peripheral. Some researchers explain this by hypothesizing that the basic instances of the extension of a term are those that have the most *visual similarity* among themselves and are the first learned by children.[5]

Intensional Gradings

While the instances of the referent can be weighted or graded as to their degree of centrality, ranging from basic to peripheral, the intension can also be graded on a basic-to-peripheral continuum. A quarter of a century ago, Achinstein advanced the notion of definitional "relevance," which is what is now being called intensional grading: "By this I mean that if an item is known to possess certain properties and lack others, the fact that the item possesses (or lacks) the property in question normally will count, at least to some extent, in favor of (or against) concluding that it is an *X*; and if it is known to possess or lack sufficiently many properties of certain sorts, the fact that the item possesses or lacks the property in question may justifiably be held to settle whether it is an *X*."[6] The characteristics that form the definitional cluster can be graded in terms of their contributions to conceptual meaning. It is in this sense that some speak of "graded conceptual structures." Some characteristics are basic or central while others are more peripheral.

Finally, it should also be noted that Achinstein's analysis includes the notion of negative relevance. For example, in the evaluation of university faculty, having a doctorate has low positive relevance, but the lack of a doctorate has high negative relevance. In other words, pointing out to an evaluation committee that a given professor possesses a doctorate will do little to increase the evaluation of that professor. But pointing out that the professor does not possess the terminal degree will lower that professor's evaluation.

Natural Categories

If we reject the idea that knowledge is that which is revealed to us about reality, we are not left with solipsism. There is an alternative view that makes room within our knowing for both individual creativity and environmental influence. Paul Churchland provides us with a neuroscientific account of how natural categories can be created.[7] He observes that we receive information from our environment by means of cells that are sensory receptors. For example, the taste of a peach begins as an activation pattern created by the four types of sensory receptor cells: sour, sweet, salty, and bitter. As Churchland notes, the power of this system can be deceptive. If one could differentiate only, say, ten levels of each of these four sensors (and some believe that this is a low estimate), then we could differentiate 10,000 distinct tastes. When we taste peach, the four specialized taste-receptor cells (sometimes called the input layer) send an excitatory/inhibitory response pattern to other target cells, by means of their synaptic connections with these cells. The target cells (sometimes called the middle layer) become activated when they detect a particular activation pattern in the input layer.

The cells that recognize sweet, sour, bitter, and salt are products of our DNA and in this sense are innately configured. But the neurons in the middle layer that recognize peaches are not created by some innate, instinctual process. Rather, the target cells are assigned by the brain to the task of detecting particular patterns that experience has indicated as important. Every one of the 10,000 possible taste-sensory input patterns does not have a target cell assigned to it. How does this allocation process take place? That is obviously an important question, and neuroscience and computer simulations will likely produce better answers. It seems to me that the process could be behavioristic, in that target cells could be assigned to sensory inputs on the basis of reinforcement. If certain molecules are present in the environment and regularly experienced by the person, then the person, by means of the process of stimulus discrimination, could learn to use this information.

As particular taste patterns assume an import of one sort or another, a taste category will be formed as an interaction between innate biological apparatus and experiencing a specific environment. In this interactive sense, natural categories could be created, with specific target cells ready to detect that specific taste pattern. What we think of as a category created in the mind could parallel the brain's assigning target cells to a particular kind of environmental input.

Note that Churchland's neuroscientific account of learning could be used to explain why researchers are detecting conceptual grading in their subjects. For example, if a child's experience with birds is for the most part with robins, then robin-detecting target cells may become common in the middle layer. For this child, robins could become the base model for the category 'bird', and be used to judge the admissibility of candidates for the category.

Eighteenth-century British empiricism held that all that we know derives from sensory data, which is a function of our sensory apparatus and gives rise to our concepts. Kant (and Piaget) criticized this "copy" theory of meaning because it did not recognize that sensory data must be assimilated or interpreted by means of mental structures to be meaningful. Behaviorists worried that the introduction of mental structures undercut the whole effort to understand learning. But if certain target cells are established to detect certain input patterns from the sensory layer, then raw sensory experience is being assimilated by means of nerve cells that have been assigned their assimilative tasks because of the experience.

The way I have presented this neuroconnectivist view of learning, especially the notion of target cells, may lead one to judge this view as overly mechanical. Churchland uses the example of a picture that is difficult to interpret, such as the abstract Christlike figure originally discussed by N. R. Hanson.[8] We can observe the picture and find no meaningful interpretation of it; yet when we are told that the picture can be understood in a certain way, our interpretation of it changes, almost with a phenomenological click. The light being received by the retina did not change, but our interpretation of that sensory input did change as a result of receiving nonvisual information. This suggests that activation patterns created in the target cells can be created or modified by the connections of the target cells with other nonsensory neurons in the network. A meaningless picture becomes cognitively meaningful because of cognitive information, not because of modifications in the light hitting the retina, that is, not because the activation pattern of the input cells has changed.

We can begin to see how we establish the properties that are the most central to the description of the extension. In Giere's terms, how do we find the basic model upon which the extension of the category is built? "What makes a basic level basic is not the internal structure of the models themselves, but the nature of various cognitive interactions between human agents and the real systems these models represent."[9] His answer clearly reveals an instrumentalist epistemology. The form of our concepts or categories does not evolve independently of the use we make of them.

Similarity Theories of Graded Structure

The existence of graded conceptual extensions and intensions is explained, for some, by the similarity view of category formation. Giere summarized this view: "In the typical account, individual real objects are classified as belonging to a particular category by their degree of similarity with an idealized object, sometimes called a 'prototype', which is defined classically by a set of necessary and sufficient features."[10] The idealized object could be either (a) a *salient feature* (a prominent member of the intension of a concept), such as having wings, or (b) an *exemplar* (a prominent member of the extension of a concept) such as robin. We could say that a category can be anchored by an exemplary member or by an important property.

Giere objects to using similarity theory as an explanation for conceptual grading. "There seems now to be considerable dissatisfaction with all similarity-based accounts of concepts. One line of criticism is that similarity accounts disregard information that seems to be part of the concept, such as that contained in correlations among relevant properties. For example, it is argued that anyone who knows what birds are knows that small birds are more likely to be song birds than large birds. Building this information into a similarity theory is difficult."[11] Note that the information disregarded by this account of concepts could be an important part of a theory of how students construct conceptual meanings.

Giere has a second concern: "A deeper objection is that similarity theories leave unexplained why some properties are relevant for a category and others not. In versions which allow some properties to count more than others, why should the weights be what they are? What holds the concept together?"[12] The traditional answer to this question has been the appeal to causal and explanatory nomological relationships. This account, the nomological net theory of scientific theories, goes as follows. Empirical generalizations emerge from human experience as natural categories. We begin to see relationships among these natural categories and, sooner or later, someone proffers a theory of why these empirical relationships have been discovered. Scientific theorizing is a high form of the science-as-refinement-of-common-sense view of scientific inquiry. Furthermore, as we attempt to develop nomological or lawlike statements by means of categories, we may find that the necessary and sufficient conditions for a given category should be modified to allow the nomological relationships that it supports to reflect the data better. In other words, the concepts of a theory are refined in light of the data. What began as an empirical generalization, a summary of a mountain of observational evidence, has its set of necessary and sufficient conditions reconstructed or reevaluated in such a way that greater weight is placed on how this set of necessary and sufficient conditions relate to other sets of necessary and sufficient conditions. Less weight is placed on the set of conditions that generated the empirical generalization in the first place. This process is sometimes referred to as making the concept in question more abstract since its meaning is pushed more toward that of other theoretical concepts and away from basic observational summaries in which it originated.

We can see why science teachers might adopt a transmissionist approach to teaching scientific concepts. If the meaning of a given concept has been abstracted within a theory to the point where everyday instances of the concept seem to be poor examples, then teachers may think it best to present the technical definition instead of beginning with familiar examples. In beginning chemistry, for example, the instances of metal that are the most interesting and useful for learning chemistry seldom resemble the substances that bicycles or automobiles are made of.

The Cognitive-Model View of Conceptual Meaning

Idealized Cognitive Models

Giere, using George Lakoff's research[13] as justification, suggests that relationships among cognitive models, not similarity of individual features, produce graded conceptual structures. Our concepts are formed around what Lakoff calls an "idealized cognitive model." This is more than an exemplary instance of the extension. The model a child may have for the concept 'worm' may be round worms common to gardens, and the model for 'bug' may be very small animals with legs. For example, the child who, when confronted with a centipede, says, "It's not a worm because it has bug feet" reveals that two models are being used to interpret what is observed.

It is this kind of overlapping of conceptual models that is at work in conceptual grading. When the more peripheral instances of the extension of a concept are examined, other concepts are brought to bear on the question, why is this instantiation of X less X-ish than other instantiations? The notion that the extension of a concept can be graded requires the importation of concepts by which the grading is performed. Every object that students can individuate is so individuated by means of several overlapping conceptual models.[14]

Vertical Grading

Vertical grading orders models for a concept in terms of their degree of abstraction. For example, Giere displayed various instances of the term 'pendulum' and ranked these to show that the term 'pendulum' serves the field of mechanics at several levels of abstraction. Assuming that researchers, such as Eleanor

Rosch, have identified the structure of the basic conceptual level, Giere holds that "becoming an expert in a science like mechanics is learning to categorize systems at levels of abstraction *above* the Roschian basic level."[15] What a novice would refer to as a "pendulum" will more than likely be seen by an expert as a member of the class of "harmonic oscillators."

This notion of vertical conceptual structuring has methodological import. If we think of conceptual analysis as an investigation of (a) extensional meaning, (b) intensional meaning, and (c) the relationships between the two (even including neuroscientific conclusions about the origin of categories), we must conclude that well-known practices of ordinary language analysis could identify most if not all of the meaning involved.

Recall that my objection to the use of the methods of ordinary language philosophy to analyze educational discourse was that it did not show us how to make use of the results of science in such analyses. The analysis of educational concepts in ordinary language, without explicit attention to how the results of science are to be used within these analyses, makes the methodology of conceptual analysis inhibitory to theoretical development. Philosophy of education should help develop our thinking, not constitute an impediment to it. In the age of neuroscience, this lack of intellectual leadership could turn out to be significant.

If the difference between a beginning student in classical mechanics and an expert in this area is the level of abstraction at which one thinks about an incline plane, pendulum, or the moon's orbit, then the methodology of conceptual analysis is provided with the means to incorporate science into its analyses. To hold the analysis of concepts at the level of ordinary discourse, is to exclude other discourses that might contribute meaning to the analyses. In the analysis of the concept of motion, we may find that by considering the meaning of 'motion' at its most abstract levels, we can better understand the thinking of students who understand motion as an object being dropped or thrown. Or, consider Kagan's research on temperament mentioned in the previous chapter. The more we know about neurological development, the more we will know about the concept of social aggressiveness. An ordinary language analysis of 'aggression' is not adequate, especially in the present age of rapidly developing neuroscience.

Conceptual Models in Educational Discourse

It may be possible to conduct studies of the category 'teaching', much as Rosch did her studies of 'bird'. Perhaps we could establish the central or basic model

Table 1. Steiner's Analysis of Metaphors

	Knowledge	Meaning	Learning
Hunter	knowledge is entity	teacher is meaning maker for others	learning is teacher-directed journey
	teacher diagnoses student needs	student is dependent	teacher predeter-mines outcomes
	student is deficient	teacher is decision maker	teacher transmits knowledge
	teacher is healer		student is container
			time is money
Britton	knowledge is world representation	learner is meaning maker	learning is student-directed experience
	language is means to curriculum	learner is independent	open-ended outcomes
	teacher creates reliable environment of interdependence and student is capable	learner is decision maker	teacher constructs knowledge with learners
	learner is scientist		student is colearner
			learner is growing plant

and several peripheral models created by bringing other models into an overlapping relationship with the basic model. While I know of no studies of 'teaching' or 'learning' that have followed Rosch's design, the work of some scholars comes close. Joan Steiner has analyzed the metaphors for knowledge, meaning, and learning found in the writings of Madeline Hunter and James Britton.[16] Table 1 has been adapted from her results.

We can imagine flashing the following sentences on a computer monitor and asking subjects to rate the sentences as *adequate* or *inadequate*.

(1) Teachers, not students, make lessons meaningful.

(2) Knowledge can be packaged into lessons and transmitted to students.

(3) Students, not teachers, make experience meaningful.

(4) Students and teacher are colearners.

Obviously, these sentences are not parallel to those used to structure the category 'bird' or 'pendulum' because subjects are partitioned by their biases for or against certain views of what teachers should do. Students trained by Hunter will judge sentences (1) and (2) adequate and (3) and (4) inadequate, whereas the opposite should occur for Britton's students.

How can we explain the fact (assuming that Steiner is correct) that Hunter and Britton use such different models to structure their concepts of teaching? It is clear that the structuring of the concept of teaching is heavily influenced by the conceptual modeling of learning, but it is also influenced by the view, even if implicit, of conceptual structures. As we have noted, if we embrace the necessary and sufficient conditions view of definitions, then it is this knowledge or meaning package that is transmitted to students, who must master the concept as presented, regardless of students' conceptual structuring prior to receiving instruction. On the other hand, if we view concepts as structured by a set of overlapping models, then the models that students bring with them into the classroom are important resources they can use to climb upwards to more abstract models. As research into the neurology of learning continues to develop, we expect that our thinking about the nature of both learning and conceptual structures will also develop.

Conceptual Models and Conceptual Analysis

Those analytical philosophers who were concerned with analyzing the methodology of language analysis sometimes mentioned "paradigm" cases as opposed to "parasitic" cases. To use what Giere calls Lakoff's favorite example, the central or basic meaning of the term 'mother' is a woman who has contributed half a child's DNA, while the term 'step mother' is parasitic on that paradigm case. Or, consider the concept of weight. 'Weight', in the sentences, 'I should lose some weight' and 'The second examination in this course has double weight' has two different meanings. The former use points to body mass, while the latter indicates a multiplicative factor of two. But we refer to this multiplicative factor as a "weighting" because the consequences of that score are heavier. The model of heavier and lighter objects is serving in these two uses of 'weight', but the weight of a brick is the model while a weighted score is a parasitic usage. This shows why ordinary language analysis worked as well as it did in many cases. But it also shows where language analysis was deficient.

Language analysis as practiced in the analytic period was deficient in two important ways. It did not (1) consider the cambium or growing edge of English, and thus was a very conservative steward of educational meaning, which can serve to inhibit the development of discourse, or (2) attend to the epistemic values inherent in any intellectual sorting of meanings, the nature of which, as we have seen, is a profound philosophic question.

If we think of English as a growing entity, we find that some terms are well entrenched over time, while others are added at a remarkable rate. English is like a meaning sponge, extracting elements from all languages it encounters.[17] (Note the effort by the French to protect their language from English.) As America becomes more and more ethnically pluralistic, one expects that American English will continue to grow as a result of meaning infusions from this cultural diversity. As more and more Americans, with diverse cultural heritages, speak English as a second language or as a companion first language, the cultural models and metaphors involved in both learning English and expressing meaning within it will increase. The analysis of English requires that we attend to what we know about the models used within various cultures. The conceptual-structures approach advocated by the naturalists is particularly well suited to the analysis of language that is undergoing rapid development.

To analyze the meaning of theoretical terms or everyday ones (and, as the notion of conceptual structuring entails, this is a quantitative not a categorical difference), we have to determine the conceptual structure of the concept by finding the various models functioning and to grade each model in terms of centrality and abstractness. This grading requires that we make use of other basic models to characterize the peripheral models as peripheral models of a given concept. Conceptual analysis becomes a kind of mapping of models, an activity that is by no means routine or algorithmic. In chapter 7, I will present an example of how the importation of meaning from other conceptual analyses can serve us in the development of educational concepts.

As ethnic diversity makes more models available to English, the question of what this or that term really means can become an issue. The articulation of specific theses about education (or most anything else) requires an intellectually legitimate form of discourse in which linguistic issues can be analyzed. What are required are normative standards for conceptual analyses. (By 'normative standards' I do not mean statistical norms or what university administrators mean by "normative data.") It is possible to claim that any discourse used to analyze language is itself political discourse and, thus, a form of political advocacy—a rather stealthy form at that.

Talk about whether the garbage is being collected, or whether the water is on, will remain functional, because of the concrete nature of its consequences, but talk in philosophy has no such anchoring. If such an anchoring is impossible, then various groups can have their own meanings, producing what Quine calls "slums of meaning." The appreciation of ethnic (and other kinds of) diversity cannot be appreciated without an adequate common discourse. I have already argued the thesis that contextualism does not have to be narrow contextualism (that philosophic pragmatism is not the same as vulgar pragmatism). However, to deal explicitly with the question of the possibility of broadly contextual discourse standards, we must consider the nature of normative inquiry, the subject of the following chapter.

For now, we see that this account of conceptual structures can help us understand (a) the relationship between theoreticians who build conceptual structures and language analysts who map them, (b) how the methodology of conceptual analysis is enhanced (perhaps dramatically) by attention to the role of models in structuring meaning, and (c) why a workable notion of normative inquiry is required to prevent conceptual anarchy.

6

NORMATIVE INQUIRY

What Is Normative Inquiry?

THE DISTINCTION BETWEEN a shopping list and a cash register receipt is a useful one for understanding the nature of normative studies. The shopping list is normative in that it gives direction to our grocery shopping, which is not an algorithmic activity but one that often requires substitutions, reevaluations, and creative additions. Price, quality, and choice are important variables that are combined with our knowledge of the culinary preferences of our family or guests and our own inventiveness. The cash register printed list, on the other hand, is a descriptive record of what was actually purchased and has no normative force for the shopper, save what dollar amount is to be recorded in the checkbook. The difference that can be sensed in the logical force of the shopping list and the cash register receipt is a difference in two types of discourse functions.

Descriptive studies of science or education are much like cash register receipts in that adequacy is a matter of representation, that is, presenting accounts of how things are, were, or will be. Studies in philosophy of science and philosophy of education are more like making shopping lists in that these inquiries strive to create normative principles that regulate the conduct of science or education by giving direction to activity through the analysis of ends, means, and their relationships. The central question is: How do we establish a principle as normative? In other words, how do we show that a principle has normative force?

Consider Dewey's distinction between the desired and the desirable.

Every person in the degree in which he is capable of learning from experience draws a distinction between what is desired and what is desirable whenever he engages in formation and choice of competing desires and interests. There is nothing far-fetched or "moralistic" in this statement. The contrast referred to is simply between the object of a desire as it first presents itself (because of the existing mechanism of impulses and habits) and the object of desire which emerges as a revision of the first-appearing impulse, after the latter is critically judged in reference to the conditions which will decide the actual result. The "desirable," or the object which *should* be desired (valued), does not descend out of the *a priori* blue nor descend as an imperative from a moral Mount Sinai. [Emphasis in original][1]

This distinction between the desired and the desirable is sometimes represented as a distinction between what is and what ought to be. Furthermore, it is often said that to confuse the *is* with the *ought* is to commit the "naturalistic fallacy." To make this distinction within a discussion of naturalistic epistemology can lead to confusion; so, let us pause for an instant and make sure we are clear on what is at issue.

Referring to the confusion of *is* and *ought* as the naturalistic fallacy is a semantical degrading of the original notion developed by G. E. Moore, which was itself not very clear. Jonathan Harrison reported on Moore's view:

> Moore contended that goodness was a unique, unanalyzable, nonnatural property [and] any attempt to define goodness in terms of any natural property must be a mistake. . . . It has been suggested that he may have meant one or other of the following: (1) The naturalistic fallacy is the fallacy of defining goodness, which is indefinable; (2) The naturalistic fallacy is not just the fallacy of defining goodness, but the fallacy of defining it in terms of natural properties and thus implying that it is a natural property; and (3) The naturalistic fallacy is the fallacy of defining goodness in terms of some property, say, happiness.[2]

The pragmatists could argue that the naturalistic fallacy is placing discourse about the desirable outside of descriptive-explanatory discourse.[3] It is clear in the Dewey comment that knowledge of the desirable (the good) begins with knowledge of the desired (the is) and is established through a process of evaluation. Moore's naturalistic fallacy was concerned with not confusing two relatively distinct discourses, not with conflating is and ought. Dewey's approach, on the other hand, is to distinguish between nonevaluated desires (desires not subjected to reflection) and evaluated ones. Why would an evaluative inquiry-generating problem occur in the first place? Unless it is simply an intellectual exercise (what is sometimes called "an academic question" because it is entertained within a context devoid of emotion or the possibility of action), the evaluative question will arise within a context of serious doubts about the desirability of something actually valued or from the problem of having to make a selection from a set of desirable alternatives. (As the late P. G. Smith used to say, the problem for philosophy is not to show us how to choose good over evil, but good over good.) In both of these evaluative situations, what is required is methodology.

If we move this discussion into the context of the methodology of conceptual analysis, the desired, or the "existing mechanism of impulse and habits," becomes the extant conceptual meaning, whether fairly clear, equivocal, ambiguous, or virtually missing. The role of conceptual analysts is to engage in critical judgment and argumentation. Existing meaning or habits must be characterized so that the object of the evaluation, the *evaluandum*, is clear or precise. The evaluation process requires certain facts and principles, the *evaluanda*, that serve to produce a justified methodology. The correct conceptual meaning is the conclusion of an evaluative argument. Note that Dewey sees the desirable emerging "as a revision" of the original *evaluandum*, thus anticipating Kaplan's distinction between the "logic-in-use" and the "reconstructed logic."[4]

Dewey's thinking provides us with a very clear interpretation of the normative character of conceptual analysis; it also shows us why simply describing extant usages does not produce conclusions about meaning that have normative force. Paul Churchland argues that the reason people do not easily give up folk psychology as an adequate interpretation of learning is because they do not want to lose the normative character of discourse about the propositional attitudes (Russell's name for belief/desire psychology).[5] The same point could be made about Kuhnian paradigms. In general, conceptual analysis deals with important values, that is, the meanings we use to describe and evaluate what we do. Conceptual analysis is inquiry which is given the task of establishing or reconstructing the content of normative discourses.

If we are to analyze a concept (or evaluate a methodology for conceptual analysis), we will have to examine these two dimensions of its use or operation. That which turns out to be desirable does not derive from some absolute, utopian conception of discourse. Communities of knowers or interpretative communities, as some like to say, must form concepts; and if these concepts are to have normative force (as opposed to being imposed though indoctrination), they will have to be evaluated. Conceptual formation and evaluation begin with a question, that is, doubt.

But how do we do this? The classic answer is that the *evaluanda* in Dewey's evaluations are "conditions and consequences," such as those presented in the following statement: "The 'desirable' as distinct from the 'desired' does not then designate something at large or *a priori*. It points to the difference between the operation and consequences of unexamined impulses and those of desires and

interests that are the product of investigation of conditions and consequences."[6] When we raise the question of consequences within the context of
normative discourse, serious philosophic problems are encountered. What
goals do we have for this discourse?

Normative Inquiry as Instrumental

One of Hilary Putnam's negative observations about Richard Rorty goes as
follows: "I think, in short, that the attempt to say that *from a God's-Eye View
there is no God's-Eye View* is still there, under all that wrapping."[7] Without en-
tering the metaphysical gap between Putnam and Rorty, we should take Putnam's remark as a caution for our thinking about methodology. If we reject
the rationalist's absolutism of the structure of the human mind and cognition, the empiricist's absolutism of analyticity, and the utopianist's "imperative from a moral Mount Sinai," then we must not, after all that, allow ourselves
to stumble into yet another absolutist conception of a priori knowledge.

The methodology of conceptual analysis is best thought of as a contextual
activity whose rules of conduct are periodically reconstructed as inquiry
moves forward. But, as we have seen, becoming free of absolutistic conceptions
of a priori knowledge is philosophic dross if we cannot avoid Hume's objections. Recall from chapter 4 that Giere's approach to establishing a naturalized
conception of normative inquiry is to focus on the "reflexive" nature of science. His strategy for solving the circular-reasoning problem was to develop
the nature of this reflexive argument. While this approach may eventually be
successful, my concern is that those epistemologists of the early part of this
century who sought to naturalize epistemology were led not to an account of
the reflexive character of science but to instrumental reasoning. The methodology for explicating the pragmatic a priori dimension of inquiry is a more
fully developed account than is Giere's reflexivity thesis. The traditional naturalist approach to the justification of scientific inferences is to be found in a
solution to the other Humean problem, that is, how do we stop the infinite
regress that seems inherent in normative arguments?

In attempting to find a justification for scientific methodology, Carl G.
Hempel was led to distinguish "methodological rationalism" and "methodological pragmatism." The former holds that "there are certain general norms
to which all sound scientific claims must conform. These are established largely
on *a priori* grounds." Hempel turned to the investigation of methodological
pragmatism because within "new perspectives provided by pragmatist studies,

scientific procedures including theory choice can still be characterized by standards that do not depend essentially on purely idiosyncratic individual factors."[8]

There are certain values and practices that are well entrenched in the experiences of scientific specialists. "Science is widely conceived as seeking to formulate an increasingly comprehensive, systematically organized, world view that is explanatory and predictive. It seems to me that the desiderata may best be viewed as attempts to articulate this conception somewhat more fully and explicitly. And if the goals of pure scientific research are indicated by the desiderata, then it is obviously rational, in choosing between two competing theories, to opt for the one which satisfies the desiderata better than its competitor." Hempel then questions whether the desiderata might, nevertheless, be idiosyncratic or subjective. He attempts to go beyond the idiosyncratic factors by what he refers to as "objectivist but 'relaxed' rational reconstruction."[9]

I take the meaning of the term 'relaxed' to be a move away from the fixed and absolute conception of the role of the a priori in science and toward a view of science in which the a priori dimension is open to refinement or reconstruction as our experience with it develops. Larry Laudan expresses a similar view; when asked about the proper goals of science, he replies: "I have no answer to give to that question, but I hasten to add—the question itself rests on illicit presumptions. There is no single 'right' goal for inquiry because it is evidently legitimate to engage in inquiry for a wide variety of reasons and with a wide variety of purposes. Those who imagine that there is a single axiology that can or should guide investigations into nature have failed to come to terms with the palpable diversity of the potential ends and uses of inquiry."[10]

Empiricists have criticized Hempel on the grounds that he cannot justify his desiderata or goals of science by using a means-end view of scientific research. They argue that the weakness in Hempel's view is that there is no way whatsoever to ground assertions about the ends or goals of science. Given a goal, one can show that certain means are adequate, but the issue involved here is to be found in the way that one can select an end or goal. The standard objection goes as follows:

> If scientific procedures and methodological norms are instrumentally efficacious with respect to scientific goals which are themselves not rational, then despite their instrumental efficacy, such procedures and norms cannot themselves be judged rational. The rationality of science goes beyond consideration of instrumental efficacy. Thus Hempel's analysis of the rationality of science will not do—not because his purported goals for science are irrational, but be-

cause his view of what that rationality consists in leaves no room for consideration of the rationality of science's goals.[11]

In other words, trying to solve the problem of the rationality of scientific methodology by appeal to the ends it serves simply drives the problem back to the unsolvable problem of the rationality of scientific goals.

Giere is obviously aware of Hempel and Laudan's thinking, but he rejects it. In a section entitled, "Can Instrumental Rationality Be Enough?" he says: "Investigating the actual goals of any group of scientists is an empirical matter, as is the investigation of the effectiveness of their means. That there is any way of evaluating the 'rationality' of these goals, apart from considering other goals to which scientific activities might be an efficient means, is problematic. That such an evaluation *must* be possible is an unproven philosophic article of faith" (emphasis in original).[12] In this conclusion he is not alone, but the rejection of the instrumental justification of scientific analyses is, I think, premature in that the classical arguments are not being fully addressed, though the thinking of some is moving in that direction.

The classical instrumentalist answer to the problem of evaluating the worth of goals is to claim that any goal must be justified instrumentally, that is, the evaluation of goals is no different from the evaluation of means. Consider Dewey's statement:

> The sole alternative to the view that *the* end is an arbitrarily selected part of actual consequences which *as* "the end" then justifies the use of means irrespective of the other consequences they produce, is that desires, ends-in-view, and consequences achieved be valued in turn as means of further consequences. The maxim referred to, under the guise of saying that ends, in the sense of actual consequences, provide the warrant for means employed—a correct position—actually says that some fragment of these actual consequences—a fragment arbitrarily selected because the heart had been set upon it—authorizes the use of means to obtain *it*, without the need for foreseeing and weighing other ends as consequences of the means used. It thus discloses in a striking manner the fallacy involved in the position that ends have value independent of appraisal of means involved and independent of their own further causal efficacy. [Emphasis in original][13]

To evaluate a goal requires examining the *means* required to reach this goal and the *consequences* of having achieved this goal. Let's consider each of these in order.

First, is it possible to realize this goal? For a goal to be actionable, it must be possible (within our epoch) to produce the goal state-of-affairs. Laudan suggests two grounds on which he could reject goal candidates: "(i) that it is uto-pian or unrealizable, or (ii) that it fails to accord with the values implicit in the communal practices and judgments we endorse."[14] It must be possible to find a means to the goal, and the goal candidate must "harmonize" with the theories being formed through the application of first-order methodology.

This reveals that Laudan is not in disagreement with what Hempel calls "methodological pragmatism," at least as far as goals may be evaluated in terms of their achievability. The two criteria Laudan mentions are actually negative criteria. A goal receives a negative evaluation if there is good evidence that it cannot be achieved, or if it does not harmonize, fit in with, or accord with other desirables. The second point suggests the pragmatic a priori in that there are some other desirables that form part of the *evaluanda* serving in the evaluation that are not in question as we evaluate this particular goal or *evaluandum*.

Second, what are the consequences of achieving the desired state of affairs? What would be the collateral consequences of acting on this goal? Showing that a given goal is realizable is necessary, but it is not sufficient. That normative inquiry is more than simply the establishment of rules for achieving ends is very clear in Dewey's remark about an objection that *he rejects*: "According to the objection, appraising applies only to *means*, while prizing applies to things that are *ends*, so that a difference must be recognized between valuation in its full pregnant sense and evaluation as a secondary and derived affair."[15] Evaluation becomes a derived and secondary affair when it is viewed as only able to evaluate means as means. The empiricists miss the potential of normative inquiry for establishing ends. Epistemology is not primary in Wittgenstein's sense, but it is not secondary and derived either.

Some will feel that in trying to evaluate a goal by examining its consequences, we simply drive the issue back to the evaluation of yet another goal. Isn't this just passing the buck? How can this approach get us anywhere? As Dewey once put the matter: "The objection always brought against the view set forth is that, according to it, valuation activities and judgments are involved in a hopeless *regressus ad infinitum*. If, so it is said, there is no end which is not in turn a means, foresight has no place at which it can stop, and no end-in-view can be formed except by the most arbitrary of acts—an act so arbitrary that it mocks the claim of being a genuine valuational-proposition."[16] If all evaluation is instrumental, then the only way to evaluate an end is as a means. But this requires another end by which to assess the first end's value as a means to the new end, and hence we have the infinite regress objection.

How can we stop this regress? To question, inquire, or investigate requires a logical place to stand from which to launch our inquiries. Empiricism sought to establish a place that would be adequate for all time, come what may in experience or sensory data. The naturalized conception of the a priori claims only that in any problem situation there will be some elements of the situation that are not in question.

Laudan accepts the conclusion of Giere and Hempel, among others, that philosophy of science must go beyond the limitations imposed by empiricist epistemology. There is currently an undeniable awareness that the rational basis of scientific inquiry may well be found in the thinking of means-ends analyses, that is, methodology/epistemological relationships. There is also a concern for the best goal-setting strategy. As Laudan makes clear, "Before a purposive action can qualify as rational, its central aims must be scrutinized . . . to see whether they satisfy the relevant constraints. But beyond demanding that our cognitive goals must reflect our best beliefs about what is and what is not possible, that our methods must stand in an appropriate relation to our goals, and that our implicit and explicit values must be synchronized, there is little more that the theory of rationality can demand."[17] This statement reveals a view of science that is contiguous with Dewey's earlier analyses of what we can expect from human thought. Note also, his statement that, "Axiology, methodology, and factual claims are inevitably intertwined in relations of mutual dependency."[18]

If the conclusion is that Laudan is properly seen as a pragmatist in the Dewey tradition, then Giere's objection that Laudan's version of metamethodology did not deal with the circularity problem loses force. Laudan's problem is Dewey's problem, namely, how to avoid an infinite regress in the justification of ends. Laudan's discussions of the role of history in the justification of scientific methodology suggests further that he views the goals of science as an instantiation of Dewey's theory of ends.[19]

Evolution or Politics?

The taken-for-granted elements in an inquiry are for the most part social, as Dewey suggests: "At any given time an adult person in a social group has certain ends which are so standardized by custom that they are taken for granted without examination, so that the only problems arising concern the best means for attaining them."[20] While some elements in every situation will be accepted, a priori, this is not to say that one may not change the context and, in that new context, question these elements. But in that new context, there will have to be some other givens—and so on it goes.

When Kuhn's conclusion that "the assent of the relevant community" is the highest standard of paradigm choice is seen in these terms, it does not turn out to be a subjective-idiosyncratic view. What else do we want from any epistemic community beyond using its composite social experience to make decisions about how to add to its knowledge? From the perspective of the static a prioris, Kuhn's remark does appear to make science subjective and arbitrary. His description of paradigm selection in *political terms* further reinforces the view that science is a political process. Giere holds that a biological analogy can be substituted for Kuhn's political analogy, thereby "invoking the notion of evolution" in the sense that there are "selective mechanisms operating on random variables."[21] I believe that this *evolutionary* interpretation of Kuhn's views is precisely the one Dewey would take were he able to address this matter. Our cognitive abilities are neither fixed in a Kantian sense nor completely flexible as Hume's view indicates; rather, our cognitive nature always has "certain tendencies already present" upon which we impose intelligence. Intelligence cannot undo what is already present. Intelligence is not subservient to what is already present. Intelligence gives direction to the development of what is already present. And how do we know what is already present? Not only do neuroscience and evolutionary psychology[22] present the extant, but they provide evidence for the warranting of claims about the best direction for further development.

Paul Churchland holds to a version of realism, but he says that we should move toward pragmatism. His reasons come from an evolutionary perspective on neuroscience, that is, the development of the brain. "There is an endless construction and reconstruction, both functional and structural. Further, it is far from obvious that truth is either the primary aim or the principle product of this activity. Rather, its function would appear to be the ever more finely tuned administration of the organism's *behavior*. Natural selection does not care whether a brain has or tends toward true beliefs, so long as the organism reliably exhibits reproductively advantageous behavior" (emphasis in original).[23] It seems more and more obvious that cognitive activity and what we think of as knowledge is better understood as something other than amassing sets of true sentences.

Recall that Dewey held that philosophic inquiry emerged when thinking became conscious of itself. This is an idealization, as was Thomas Hobbes's notion of primitive peoples forming a social compact, but it does give us an evolutionary perspective. What would be evaluated is behavior, conduct, habits, and social customs. Before the brain developed to the point where thinking could become conscious of itself, nature evaluated behavior, and in harsh terms. Surviving attributes were stored in the DNA, but when the human brain emerged, it became possible for people to engage in evaluation and to anticipate consequences from present and imagined conditions before nature evaluated actual human behavior.

Many of those who reject modernism reject evolutionary theory as part of it, but Darwin and Wallace[24] are just as much part of the criticism of the "autonomous self" as Freud; moreover, the evolutionists have done more than Freud to explicate the violent, dominant, and sexual aspects of human nature. That this work can simply be assigned to the category "modernism" and then dismissed in favor of a political model of cognitive and affective development is itself a move in a political process. If scientific development is to be seen as a political process, then 'political' must mean something it doesn't mean in Washington. Laudan observes, "The history of science does not generally appear to be the history of factions arbitrarily banished from science. In most scientific controversies, the proponents of the losing side come eventually, and often enthusiastically, to embrace the views, and sometimes even the aims, of the victors—scarcely what we would expect if their 'conversion' were forced or strained."[25]

When the famous paradigm shift occurs, the old and new paradigms are what Kuhn calls incommensurable. The nature of incommensurability continues to be the focus of much analysis, but it is true to Kuhn's position to say that the shift involves both changes in meaning (linguistic adequacy) and in methodological standards (extralinguistic adequacy). Giere makes the following observation: "Laudan argues that we can get from one paradigm to another in a series of steps, each of which is instrumentally rational, and not, as Kuhn claimed, in one, nonrational leap of faith. The appearance of the global paradigm change in historical cases is, Laudan argues, an artifact of too distant a historical perspective. Looking more closely, he claims, we see smaller, more piecemeal changes."[26] Laudan is definitely taking an instrumentalist approach to the justification of scientific knowledge; moreover, the above statement suggests that Laudan is making use of the continuity principle when he concludes that paradigm shifts reflect more continuity than Kuhn's interpretations of history suggest.

This is an issue within epistemological naturalism whose importance should not be underestimated; it is not, however, an issue that bears directly on the philosophic legitimacy of naturalism. Pragmatists of the preanalytic period always looked at experience as having a certain amount of unpredictability about it, which means that while we should strive to maintain intellectual continuity with previous thought, we should be aware that there will always be developments that are not predictable and can radically change our way of thinking and acting.

Within the strict or classic view of Kuhn's claims, the paradigm shift is a leap of faith, as Giere puts it, and, as Laudan notes further, what was all controversy and disagreement becomes, after the shift, general agreement. This agreement occurs quickly and some of the paradigm's critics become its advocates in a short time. The political community view of scientific inquiry is challenged by Laudan's observation. Changing points of view in science and politics seem to be quite different processes.

I think that the pragmatist's point should be made that while the paradigm shift of meaning and standards is drastic, it, nevertheless, takes place within a context of undoubted belief. When Einstein's predictions of the eclipse proved more accurate than the established view with which he disagreed, his view came to be the accepted one, but we continued to use the telescopes that were built before the special theory of relativity was considered warranted. The point is that during a paradigm change, not everything changes; the change occurs within a context of the unchanged.

What Are the Goals of Conceptual Analysis?

Paul Churchland has argued that what he called the "superempirical virtues" are more important for scientific theories than being true to the data.

> As I see it, values such as ontological simplicity, coherence, and explanatory power are some of the brain's most basic criteria for recognizing information, for distinguishing information from noise. And I think they are even more fundamental values than is "empirical adequacy," since collectively they can overthrow an entire conceptual framework for presenting the empirical facts. Indeed, they even dictate how such a framework is constructed by the questing infant in the first place. One's observational taxonomy is not read off the world directly; rather, one comes to it piecemeal and by stages, and one settles on that taxonomy which finds the greatest coherence and simplicity in the world, and the most and the simplest lawful connections.[27]

These "superempirical virtues" are often called pragmatic values because they refer to the knower's psychology, but if Churchland and Giere are right, they are not arbitrary human values because they emerge from analysis of our neuroform.

I see this as a clear instantiation of Dewey's account of the instrumental nature of normative argumentation. The methodology we call scientific inquiry is a means to an end, that is, scientific knowledge, and as our discussion suggests, just what this end is is hotly debated in philosophy of science. Applying instrumental evaluation to scientific methodology requires that we have some account of the ends of science by which the methodology can be evaluated. This is the Hempelian point. But how do we know which ends to use to warrant the methodology in question? Dewey's answer is to evaluate these proposed ends in terms of their consequences, which is to say, treat these ends to be evaluated as if they were means. At this point, philosophy of science lugged, as it were, and found it difficult to make progress. Churchland and Giere have argued that neuroscience cannot be ignored in these debates, and while Giere has doubts about instrumental reasoning, Churchland shows us that there is a way to evaluate the goals of science. He appeals to what is known about neurological development to defend simplicity, for example, as a warranted goal. Neurodevelopment, both ontological (individual) and phylogenetic (species), provides a source for evaluation. This suggests that evolutionary theory and neuroscience are essential elements in contemporary epistemology. Note that this evaluation is a matter of shifting the context of evaluation. By shifting from the evaluation of methodology in terms of ends to the evaluation of the ends, we moved the discussion into the context of cognitive science. Giere is worried about circularity, but the pragmatist distinction between the doubted and the undoubted contextualizes this problem.

This gives direction to the question of goals for inquiry. Note that his appeal to simplicity, coherence, and explanatory power are desiderata that can serve as general targets within inquiry, which can be evaluated in terms of their consequences. Just as Churchland finds empirical correspondence insufficient for accepting a theory, we find descriptive adequacy within ordinary language analysis an insufficient goal or desideratum. An adequate conceptual analysis must actively pursue, inter alia, discourse simplicity, coherence, and explanatory power.

This suggests, further, that to do conceptual analysis, one must have inquiry goals that give direction to the enterprise. I believe that a quantitative distinction can be made between (a) the conceptual development process that is a necessary part of theory construction, and (b) conceptual analysis as conducted in philosophy. When a scientist modifies a definition in light of the other concepts of a theory or creates original definitions, the process he or she is engaged in has the goal of making the theory more adequate. The concept is developed as a part of a larger whole that will be evaluated, which means that the norms for judging adequacy are remote. For philosophers, the evaluation is more immediate and direct because the concept being analyzed is considered in light of the norms that should be satisfied. The larger whole is a discourse, not a theory. Conceptual analysis within cognitive science is often more like philosophy than normal science because the epistemic virtues are frequently well in mind as the analysis progresses.

If readers go back to the philosophy of education literature of the analytical period and examine the analyses of concepts taken to be significant in educational discourse, they will find that it is not at all clear just what desiderata were being pursued. The analytical equivalent of empirical adequacy, actual usage, seems to be the standard of adequacy, yet there was talk about improving educational discourse. What were missing, among other things, were the cognitive values mentioned above.

The Aesthetic Dimension of Cognitive Growth

Recall that within any problematic situation, there are many elements that are not in question. The question of additional effects of the means used and the question of consequences of achieving the end are questions designed to lead us to examine how the consequences of our actions will fit into the larger value context. If the projected goal will fill the void or lack that was detected when we first became aware of the problematic nature of the situation, then by considering the three relationships mentioned, we are evaluating how well this goal will restore equilibrium.

Removing the lack or deficit that led to the creation of the desire, through problem-solving, should be seen as part of a continuing dynamic state in which we find ourselves. As Dewey argued, it is a sign of immaturity when a person fails to see a goal as "a moving condition for further consequences, thereby treating it as *final* in the sense in which 'final' signifies that the course of events has come to a complete stop." He goes on to say that we "do indulge in such arrests," but to treat such pauses as a model for a "theory of ends" would be a serious mistake.[28] The forming and pursuing of goals is a constant and fluid process within which the exercise of intelligence is found.[29]

Part of the explanation for some philosophers' thinking that instrumental value theory is not dealing with the real value questions stems from the assumption that any adequate theory of value would produce values or principles that are absolute, in the sense that they must apply to all contexts in which people find themselves. The search for such values is bound to lead to the real infinite regress, regress into complete skepticism and cynicism. But if we give up the quest for valuational certainty, that is, free ourselves from the pursuit of the absolute and the resultant feelings of inadequacy when we cannot find it, we can be much more open to the features of the actual situations in which we find ourselves. Our intellectual resources are liberated. Acting intelligently in life requires knowing, first, that which can be held come what may in this situation, and, second, what should be carefully evaluated in terms of means and consequences. In this sense, moral theory is no different from scientific theory. Scientific knowledge comes to us as a refinement of common sense, in that scientific inquiry begins with what is accepted and subjects it to further analysis. Inquiry takes place within a paradigm or framework that is not itself questioned in normal times. If the inquiry is frequently frustrated, then the paradigm will come under review.

One might begin to wonder about the completeness of this theory of evaluation because of its focus on solving problems that derive from obstacles or lacks in what we are already doing prior to the realization of the problematic situation. The theory appears to be solely remedial in nature. This is not at all the case. Robert Westbrook pointed out that, Dewey

> readily acknowledged that the moral life required much that science and philosophy could not offer. There was more to the pursuit of happiness, justice, and virtue than good judgment, which could draw only on past experience. If valuing consisted wholly of inquiry and adjudication then it would be cut off from the untried possibilities of experience, which could only be imagined. Imagination was the chief instrument of the good, and Dewey believed that artists, not philosophers, were the most significant, if often unconscious, trustees of the moral imagination.[30]

Art begins with the familiar and presents it to us so that we see new, complete or unified possibilities for it. The settled present does not always become problematic because something therein fails or wears out. Through imagination the settled can be threatened, thinking can be provoked into the creation of new goals, and desires can be mobilized into the action to make them real. It is in this aesthetic sense that ideas are emergent and not fully predictable.

Instrumentalism or Utopianism?

Instrumental value theory requires scientific content, which leads First Philosophy to consider it unacceptable. While instrumentalism is faring no better than empiricism with the political ideologues, there is reason to think that its reconsideration is important.

Albrecht Wellmer, in his book *The Persistence of Modernism*, identifies two streams of postmodernism.

> With the 'death of God' virtually forgotten, the contemporary postmodernist debate frequently proclaims the 'death of modernity' instead. . . . And not withstanding the variety of interpretations brought to bear on the subject, the death of modernity is invariably conceived as something entirely warranted: it is seen as the termination of a terrible mistake, a collective madness, a relentless compulsion, a deadly illusion. The obituaries for modernity are often full of sarcasm, bitterness and hatred. Never has a project that began with such a proliferation of good intentions—I mean the project of European Enlightenment—had such obloquy muttered over its grave.[31]

But as he further points out, not all advocates of postmodernism have claimed that modernity is dead; for these thinkers, modernity is undergoing a transformation, and they are concerned with the issue of whether (a) it will acquire "a more advanced consciousness of itself" or (b) it will regress socially as the information age pours down around us and controlling information becomes the factor on which culture and politics is centered (in Piaget's sense).

I claim that this is an important issue for philosophy of education today. Wellmer frames the matter by his conclusion that "The critique of instrumental reason cannot do without a philosophy of history based on the idea of reconciliation; it needs a utopian perspective because it would cease to be conceivable as a *critique* otherwise."[32] The postmodernists want to fill the intellectual vacuum left by empiricism with a utopian view of the self, science, and society. If Wellmer is correct, the current pursuit of utopianism makes sense, because both the empiricists and the utopians share the belief that empiricism is the proper replacement of instrumentalism, and the utopians believe that they are the successors to empiricism. My thesis is that both of these judgments are epistemologically hasty.

Democracy and Education was published in 1916 (one year before the birth of the former Soviet Union). In this book, Dewey clearly rejects utopian conceptions of social progress because they ignore the principle of continuity of experience. Utopian approaches seek to start over, as it were, by rejecting wholesale all of what came before. A central feature of such rejection is the attempt to purify speech by eradicating our semantic endowments. Even if it were possible to do so, and the history of the English language throws doubt on the idea, the pragmatic conception of a priori knowledge shows us that to do so would be a type of cognitive lobotomy.

Dewey argued that when utopian ideas are set in motion, we can never know that these ideas will be effective. "We cannot set up out of our heads, something we regard as an ideal society. We must base our conception upon societies which actually exist, in order to have any assurance that our ideal is a practicable one."[33] The description of a utopian state, no matter how extensive the literature, can never describe every dimension of every practical problem that will arise. And when major changes in social policy occur, new practical problems will emerge. The social experience of a society serves as a resource for solving many practical problems, but if this experience is rejected, practical problems must be faced often without insight. Societies built on what seem to be adequate theoretical ideas will encounter numerous practical problems that will prove devastating in composite. In pursuing utopian ideas, we must reject so much of the present that we do not have sufficient experience to deal with the surfeit of sub-theoretical problems that we will encounter. In other words, when we consciously reject the continuity of human experience, as pursuits of utopias so eagerly do, we deprive ourselves of significant resources by drastically limiting the a priori knowledge to which we can appeal when faced with serious problems.

Once an absolute commitment is made to substantive material claims, the methodology for establishing pragmatic a priori knowledge derived from human experience is replaced by a fixed and certain conception of how the universe should be. All subsequent "scientific" effort is then devoted to showing that this previously accepted view, one not susceptible of evaluation or reconstruction, must be the correct one. This view is the fourth conception of a priori knowledge—the substantive a priori, or better still, Lysenkoism.

T. D. Lysenko was an influential biologist of the former Soviet Union, who, along with his colleagues, "rejected the gene theory on *a priori*, abstract considerations, ignoring the factual material of genetics. They attempted to abolish genetics on the grounds that it was an allegedly formalistic, bourgeois, and metaphysical science, and to inaugurate their own new genetics."[34] Why did

Lysenko reject genetics as a legitimate area of scientific research? Within the ideology of utopianism, as Zhores Medvedev further points out, "Engels advanced his famous theoretical study of the role of work in the process of transformation of ape into man—the transmissibility of characteristics acquired through food and exercise. It should be noted that Engles did not reinforce his assumption by any strictly verified facts. It must be taken into account that Engels' work belongs to a period before genetics as a science of heredity existed."[35] Lysenko argued, on the basis of the thesis of the transmissibility of acquired traits, that wheat would adapt to the Soviet climate. This contradicts the genetic theory, which holds that changes in the wheat will occur only by genetic mutations. (The technology of genetic engineering did not yet exist.) Wheat cannot learn from its climatic experience, which is what Lysenko was, in effect, claiming.

Lysenko recognized that research in genetics was rapidly developing and that he must answer it. To protect socialist science, Lysenko held that the gene theory was a bourgeois notion that had to be rejected to make progress. Unfortunately, as Medvedev observes, this defense involved "Distortion of facts, demagoguery, intimidation for their ideas, reliance on authorities, eye wash, misinformation, self-advertising, repression, obscurantism, slander, fabricated accusation, insulting name calling, and physical elimination of opponents—all were part of the rich arsenal of effective means by which, for nearly thirty years, the 'progressive' nature of scientific concepts were confirmed."[36] Medvedev further states that there is,

> sufficient proof of Lysenkoism's bankruptcy, of its detachment from world science, of its sectarian nature. The analysis also shows that it is impossible to fight Lysenkoism by methods of academic discussion and scientific argument. Lysenkoism does not recognize any criticism from without, any critique by representatives of other scientific trends.
>
> We have shown here how Lysenkoism attained its supremacy, and this we consider the most important point. Only a scientifically bankrupt doctrine would use such methods; correct theories spread and win recognition primarily because they are correct. False concepts can be imposed temporarily on science only by demagoguery, repression, and suppression; correct ideas and theories develop and find support in spite of any suppressive methods. *The demonstration of the ways and means that secured the imposition of Lysenkoism on our science for so long is, then, a demonstration of its scientific bankruptcy.*
>
> We have paid particular attention to the fate of many scientists who per-

ished tragically during the period of the personality cult because of their participation in the debate described. [Emphasis in original][37]

Lysenko and his associates adopted the ideological conception of a priori knowledge. When any of the scientific content of this a priori is challenged, there is no epistemological defense possible because this a priori knowledge did not derive from any epistemological process. As a child of sociopolitical theory, this a priori knowledge must be accepted *in toto* because there is no mechanism for its reconstruction or reevaluation. Critics must be enemies because the only explanation of criticism is false consciousness. All critics must be silenced to protect the a priori commitments on which the theory of progress is based. Utopias are not built on doubt. Epistemologically speaking, critics are dealt with harshly not out of meanness, but because there is no methodological possibility of their being correct. We can only have conversations with those who share our absolute assumptions (as one-sided a view of "conversation" as we can think of). If criticism is so vocal and disruptive, then reeducation or banishment is the only alternative.

In his book on the fall of the former Soviet Union, *The Grand Failure*,[38] Zbigniew Brzezinski makes the following observation about social control: "The essence of totalitarian rule is the elimination of any autonomous political life and the atomization of society. The objective is to make certain that every individual is left alone to face the system as a whole, feeling isolated and often adrift in his or her internal but never publicly expressed opposition." In Poland, the movement that emancipated itself from such totalitarian rule named itself *Solidarnosc*—Solidarity. Brzezinski continues, "Solidarity conveyed the very opposite message. It signaled a new reality of shared consciousness, of collective confidence, and of an alliance between different social strata or classes."[39]

The distance between Lysenko-like thought in American philosophy of education and Dewey's ideas cannot be overemphasized. Consider Dewey's view of the nature of social groups. "There is honor among thieves, and a band of robbers has a common interest as respects its members. Gangs are marked by fraternal feeling, and narrow cliques by intense loyalty to their own codes. . . . Now in any social group whatever, even a gang of thieves, we find a certain amount of interaction and cooperative intercourse with other groups." But how should we develop "a measure for the worth of any given form of social life," as Dewey put it? His two classic but underappreciated questions emerge: "How numerous and varied are the interests which are consciously shared? How full and free is the interplay with other forms of association?"[40] Dewey appeals to the example of a criminal organization.

> We find that the ties which consciously hold the members together are few in
> number, reducible almost to a common interest in plunder; and they are of
> such a nature as to isolate the group from other groups. . . . In order to have a
> large number of values in common, all members of the group must have an
> equal opportunity to receive and to take from others. There must be a large
> variety of shared undertakings and experiences. Otherwise, the influences
> which educate some into masters, educate others into slaves.[41]

I submit that this emphasis on open interaction with other forms of associa-tion separates Dewey's concept of democracy and creates a measure of social worth that is different from that held by many writing in philosophy of edu-cation today.

No Doubts, No Progress

The instrumentalist view of the individual-society relationship considers the individual problem-solvers to be the growing edge—the cambium—from which improvement emerges. The utopian view of the individual-society rela-tionship sees the continuity principle as an anchor that must be jettisoned if social progress is to be realized. This sets instrumentalism and utopianism in diametric opposition.

The role of doubt is central to this separation. The utopians encourage doubt in thought about modernism but prohibit it within discourse about the utopia. By freeing them from their doubts about the utopian characterization, utopianism empowers students to take part in society and reap its benefits. If they continue to harbor doubts, they must be reeducated, by attending various social therapy experiences. This contrasts sharply with Dewey's methodology, which thrives on doubt. Everything cannot be doubted at once, but everything can be doubted. To engage in inquiry, thus, requires us to make prioritizing judgments. The utopians and the pragmatists have quite different attitudes to-ward contrary views.

After Kuhn's historical analysis of scientific development became a cen-tral topic in epistemology and philosophy of science, the utopians took Kuhn's conclusion that there were no methodological principles that transcended the judgments of the community of inquirers to mean that any group could make up their own rules. Kuhn's thesis seems to have been interpreted by the utopians as giving them epistemic license. If there is no God, then come, let us join together and be God! The utopians view the emphasis of logical empiricism on logical structure and rational foundation as not being able to address the organic problems of human experience; moreover, they view ordinary language philosophy as being so overly pious toward our semantical endowment that it is unable to envision a discourse capable of describing problems and solutions to our problems. Assuming that all philosophy of the twentieth century is empiricistic, the utopians turned away from philosophic inquiry, holding that it was serving to legitimate the status quo. What was required was a discourse that was free of modernism's semantical endowment, an alternative that they set out to create in the literature and, through reacculturation, in the minds of the young. Equipped with a belief that they knew what was both true and moral, the present-day Lysenkos formed a new corpus of meaning and began to use their professional power and institutional status to indoctrinate the young into it.

Tina Rosenberg, in her 1995 National Book Award–winning account of Europe after communism, makes the following observation:

> Fascism espouses repugnant ideas, but communism's ideas of equality, solidarity, social justice, an end to misery, and power to the oppressed are indeed beautiful. The New Socialist Man—tireless, cheerful, clean, brave, thrifty, and kind to animals—is an ideal all humanity should aspire to reach. The problem, as even believing Communists admit, is that this utopian landscape must be stocked with ordinary people. Communism is lofty and grand, but human beings are flawed creatures, unwilling to pay communism the tribute of sacrifice it demands.[42]

Utopian conceptions cannot provide moral leadership by dropping a moral code on us "out of the *a priori* blue" or "as an imperative from a moral Mount Sinai" and then setting out to find a science to confirm it. Science and philosophy are sustained by doubt; they cannot long exist without real and living doubt. Instrumentalists are always seeking new problems to solve and, in turn, often reexamining the undoubted in inquiry. It was the pragmatists who saw science as a contributor of meaning, as an antecedent to meaning, not its consequent. It was they who saw that scientific growth will eventually produce fissures in any rigid vessel. The organic, evolutionary nature of thought will not long be served by a fixed set of categories, and if we are to understand science and give direction to it, we must achieve an epistemology oriented toward growth, not certainty. Science should add to the meaning of our experience and increase our ability to direct the course of subsequent scientific experience. (This is Giere's point about the role of cognitive science in understanding science.) No mind or group of minds is great enough to devise a fixed or certain framework that can serve for long to make experience intelligible. The history of pragmatism in the twentieth century is the history of efforts to free our thinking from the search for absolute, decontextualized frameworks. Experience is made intelligible through processes that not only permit doubt, but embrace and encourage it.

7

IS TEACHING A CAUSAL PROCESS?

Naturalized Conceptual Analysis

AN ADEQUATE METHODOLOGY of conceptual analysis must be able to integrate the results of science into the explication of conceptual meaning. Kagan's recent research was cited as an example of this approach to conceptual analysis (see chapter 4). But Salmon's analysis of causation provides us with an example of conceptual analysis being used within the context of a traditional (and resistant) philosophic problem. In this chapter, I want to review Salmon's analysis of causation (especially the way it draws meaning from physics) and apply the results of his analysis to educational discourse concerned with the nature of teaching.

Philosophy of education focuses on the philosophic aspects of human development, teaching, and the social institutions designed to support both. As we have seen, philosophy of education as conducted during the analytic period did not focus on learning and human development because this domain was seen primarily as an empirical one and was thus not amenable to First Philosophy's science-free approach. On the other hand, everyday speech contains very little information about human development and effective teaching, and if the anti–folk-psychology philosophers are correct, the content that it does contain is misleading. The study of human development was seen as educational psychology, and the related philosophic studies were devoted to the analysis of values implicit in the various theories of learning and human development. Surprisingly little attention was paid to the epistemological dimension of this discourse or to evaluating the methodologies of educational psychology in light of the discussions in philosophy of science.

The study of teaching did not fare much better under empiricism. The First Philosophy approach to teaching was limited to discussions of rational teaching—as if we could talk intelligently about what is rational in this world without the knowledge of how this world fits together. The ordinary language analysis of 'teaching' extracted about all of the meaning that was to be had; but, as I noted, even with that meaning established, we have to wonder about the value of these analyses for the education profession in light of the arguments of those who doubt folk psychology.

The epistemological naturalists reject the approach to conceptual analysis developed by First Philosophy and claim that the results of science must be considered if we are to achieve adequate conceptions of what we are about. Readers might rightly say that it is high time naturalists put up their case and show us how to use science in conceptual analysis. The most basic philosophic problem in the philosophy of teaching is the notion of teacher effects. Without a clear idea of what it means to have an effect, talk about (a) teacher effectiveness, (b) the proper goals of teaching, and (c) a professional code of ethics for teachers is going to be ambiguous and possibly misleading.

University programs that prepare professional educators, state licensure procedures, and the expectations of many parents are all predicated on the belief that competent practitioners can have an *effect* on students. Taxpayers agree to spend millions each year because of their belief that schools can *influence* children. Classroom teachers are often judged on how well they *produce* academic desiderata. Yet educational researchers, who are ostensibly building the knowledge base for teaching, speak only of independent and dependent variables and of how some variance is associated with other variance. Why hasn't philosophy of science given philosophy of teaching more to work with?

Bertrand Russell, one of the great philosophers of the twentieth century, told researchers that advanced sciences simply do not use the term 'cause'.[1] Talk of causes and effects might well denote an inchoate (or even a poorly developing) science. Perhaps we are better advised, as Philip G. Smith claims, to speak of "invariant associations" instead of cause-effect relationships.[2] This view of the role of causality in science originates with, and faithfully follows, David Hume.

> Here is a billiard ball lying on the table, and another ball moving toward it with rapidity. They strike; the ball which was formerly at rest now acquires a motion. This is as perfect an instance of the relation of cause and effect as any which we know either by sensation or reflection. Let us therefore examine it. It is evident that the two balls touched one another before the motion was communicated, and that there was no interval betwixt the shock and the motion. *Contiguity* in time and place is therefore a requisite circumstance to the operation of all causes. It is evident, likewise, that the motion which was the cause is prior to the motion which was the effect. *Priority* in time is, therefore, another requisite circumstance in every cause. But this is not all. Let us try any

other balls of the same kind in a like situation, and we shall always find that the impulse of the one produces motion in the other. Here, therefore, is a *third* circumstance, namely, that of *constant conjunction* betwixt the cause and the effect. Every object like the cause produces always some object like the effect. Beyond these three circumstances of contiguity, priority, and constant conjunction I can discover nothing in this cause.[3]

This argument that cause-effect reasoning has no cognitive merit has been so intimidating that many have accepted its conclusion in spite of the fact that professional shop talk and claims made in many professional publications obviously rest on a contrary belief.

Recent work in the theory of scientific explanation has produced a well-developed conception of causality, the most basic one yet devised; this concept is significant for the philosophic study of teaching. Wesley Salmon has recently argued that it is possible to characterize causal explanations ("putting the cause back in because," as he says) in science and that these explanations are an essential feature of scientific thinking.[4] Though he would not like my saying so, he presents a paradigm case for naturalistic studies. How so? Salmon's concept of causation is drawn from the special theory of relativity. The argument is somewhat involved, and I will not attempt to summarize it here; my point is that Salmon's powerful statement on the nature of causation is grounded in a scientific theory—albeit a very comprehensive one. It is no stretch of language, meaning, or semantics to say that Salmon's analysis of causation and causal explanation is a naturalized one in that it is a counterexample to the wisdom of First Philosophy's avoidance of the use of scientific findings in philosophic analysis. Salmon makes a profound philosophic point about the nature of scientific inquiry by making a fundamental appeal to the results of science.

Causal Explanation

To understand Salmon's account of causation, it is necessary to take a brief journey into the matter of scientific explanation. It was Salmon's investigations of the nature of scientific explanation that led him to reopen the case on causation, one long thought closed by Hume. It is commonly recognized that the two most central problems in philosophy of science are scientific inference and scientific explanation. The study of scientific explanation began in 1948 with the classical Carl Hempel and Paul Oppenheim paper, "Studies in the Logic of Explanation," in which what is known as the "covering law" theory was advanced.[5] To explain an event, the *explanandum*, it must be subsumed under scientific laws, the *explanans*. A consequence of the covering-law thesis is Hempel's famous "symmetry thesis," which views explanation and prediction as differing only in time, that is, whether or not the event has occurred.

In what Hempel calls "deductive-nomological" explanations, the *explanans* consist of (a) one or more scientific laws, (b) a statement of conditions, and (c) deductive inference rules. Hempel recognized that some laws may be statistical and that statistical laws can produce statistical explanations. Since statistical propositions cannot produce deductive-nomological explanations, Hempel identified "inductive-statistical" explanations, which confer a high probability on the *explanandum*. Including statistical explanations in the covering-law theory made it a more comprehensive account of scientific explanation, but it contained a controversial characteristic, that is, when an improbable event occurs, the standard thesis must consider it unexplainable. Hempel's standard covering-law thesis explains events by showing that the event was expected.

Salmon considers the whole area of statistical explanation surprisingly underdeveloped in the philosophy of science literature and has presented an account of statistical explanation that allows for the explanation of improbable occurrences. Salmon's thesis is that to explain improbable events we have to have an account of scientific explanation that makes use of the concept of causation because to explain improbable events requires correctly placing them within causal patterns. Hempel's covering-law version of scientific explanation takes the point of scientific inquiry to be the discovery of invariant associations and seeks to construct explanations in terms of these associations. Salmon disagrees: "If, however, we adopt the view that the point of an explanation is to exhibit events as having their places in patterns, and accept the notion that some of the patterns are irreducibly statistical patterns, then the explanation of the low-probability event seems just as natural and acceptable as that of the high probability event, for the stochastic pattern is one that includes events of both types."[6]

Two points are important: (a) the adequacy of beliefs about causation implicit in professional educational discourse can now be addressed in ways that throw new light on professional education; (b) the philosophic warrant or legitimation to which Salmon appeals in his theory can be used to further refine our ideas about the nature of conceptual analysis in the postanalytic philosophic period.

Causal Processes Versus Pseudo-Processes

Though he does not present a rigorous definition of 'process', Salmon shifts the focus of discussions of causality from event ontology to causal processes. From the time of Hume on, we have thought about cause-effect reasoning as a relationship between or among events, but Salmon claims that this has obscured what is at issue. He views causality as a relationship among processes and claims that the special theory of "relativity demands that we make a distinction between *causal processes* and *pseudo-processes*."[7]

How could the special theory of relativity be relevant to the philosophic question of the nature of cause-effect relationships? How could a scientific theory of the physical universe be instructive to philosophic thought about teaching or conceptual analysis? Of course, on the First Philosophy view it could not possibly do so, but for epistemological naturalists the relationship is not at all surprising. The distinction between a causal process and a pseudo-process is that causal processes possess the ability to transmit a mark; this difference is fundamental to Salmon's theory and, I think, to considerations of its legitimacy. It thus behooves us to take the time required to understand it.

According to relativity theory, light is the *first signal*, which means that no causal process can exceed the speed of light in a vacuum. I think it was Russell who said that when someone claims that "everything is relative," we have the right to ask, "to what?" If we ask, "to what?" in relativity theory, the answer is light. The speed of light is an absolute, even though we occasionally read about processes that are said to exceed the speed of light. For example, imagine a laser device on Earth aimed at Jupiter. When the laser is activated, we can produce a dot on the Jovian surface. Furthermore, imagine that this laser is capable of rapid rotations, and that we can make the dot on Jupiter move across the surface of the planet. We determine the speed of rotation of the laser that is required to make the laser dot sweep across the Jovian surface at just the speed of light. (Note that the laser device does not have to move at the speed of light, because its movement through a short arc may be quite slow when compared with the speed of the dot on the Jovian surface. The Earth motion may be a few millimeters while the motion of the dot on Jupiter will travel thousands of meters in the same time interval.)

Now consider an object in space that is twice the distance from Earth as Jupiter. At what speed will the laser dot sweep that object? Obviously, if the dot on the Jovian surface is moving at the speed of light, then the dot that sweeps the object farther away must be moving faster than the speed of light because the dot must traverse a much greater distance. This is a reasonable thought experiment, but has it uncovered a flaw in the special theory of relativity, just as Russell discovered a contradiction in set theory? Not at all. There are many examples in the literature describing processes that exceed the speed of light, but these processes are not causal processes. Recall that for a process to be a causal process it must be able to produce a mark. If it cannot, it is a pseudo-process. As you have now guessed, the dot sweeping Jupiter and the other object in space is a pseudo-process.

One might object that this is nothing more than an *ad hoc* distinction concocted to save the theory from an obvious counterexample. To the contrary, it is a fundamental idea in the way twentieth-century scientists think about space. Light's first signal status is not refuted by these examples of processes that exceed it because these processes are not signals. A signal can carry a mark, that is, information. The laser dot moving across the Jovian surface cannot be used to transmit information. This is the central notion in the conception of causation being presented.

That light can be used as a signal is obvious to anyone who has ever flashed their automobile's headlights. For years, ships at sea used an interruptible light source and a common signal system to communicate with other vessels. Paul Revere left a light in the tower of the Old North Church, and our laser device mounted on Earth could transmit a signal to an astronaut on Jupiter, perhaps by pulsing the laser in long and short intervals or by intermittently placing a barrier between the light and the Jovian surface.

So why can't the laser's dot traversing the Jovian surface be a signal? As children, we looked out of car windows and watched the shadow of the car run parallel to the car's line of travel. If the sun was at the correct angle, we could wave to ourselves. When the car went past a solid fence, we noticed the shape change so that the bottom part of the shadow remained on the ground but the upper portion was bent upward at what was close to a right angle. The shadow was modified by the landscape. Could we use this modification to transmit information?

Let's say that Joe's house is next to a railroad track. A friend of his lives a few miles farther down these same tracks. Every day, just at noon, a freight train passes Joe's house. Can Joe communicate with his friend by means of the train's shadow? Joe erects a wooden structure, so that when the train passes his house the train's shadow is changed in some way. (A large piece of plywood could be erected to block the light between two boxcars so that just at that point, the shadow appears to reflect one boxcar that is twice the length of the others.) Joe's friend knows the code and when the train's shadow reaches him in a modified state, it means that Joe can go to the movie that afternoon.

We shake our heads at this communication plan because it is sadly out of touch with the facts of the world. Yes, we can change shadows by changing the landscape, but these changes are not able to communicate information. Why? If the two friends had devised a different system, the communication would work. Suppose that Joe obtains a small ball of soft mud and throws it against the first boxcar in the train. His friend could examine the appropriate side of the first boxcar and receive a signal. Let us be clear on this difference. The wooden device that modified the train's shadow made a change that was not sustainable, but the clay that sticks to the boxcar is a sustainable change. The train's shadow cannot sustain its mark, but the mud dot on the boxcar is sustainable, except in the case of rain. The dot on the Jovian surface is in the same category as the train's shadow; it cannot sustain a mark. The dot or the shadow cannot transmit information because both are dependent on the laser's or the sun's light, respectively, which makes the moving dot and the shadow pseudo-processes. Pseudo-processes are parasitic on causal ones.

Causal Production Versus Causal Propagation

What I have just been describing in terms of a process's ability to sustain a mark is described by Salmon in different terms. Let's broaden the notion of sustainability by considering his distinction between production and propagation. As Salmon points out, while "causal production and causal propagation are intimately related to one another," we should not attempt "to reduce one to the other."[8] What is this difference? Causal processes can create (produce) a mark, for example, when mud is thrown against a boxcar or when children carve their initials into the base of a baseball bat with a pocket knife. These initials are marks that result from the causal process of carving with a knife.

A causal process is self-propagating in that it can retain its mark, which is why causal processes can transmit information and pseudo-processes cannot. Both the train's shadow and the baseball bat were modified or changed by causal production. The train's shadow, however, is a pseudo-process because it could not propagate the change. Shadows cannot propagate their marks and thus cannot serve as signals. The bat, however, retains its marks because it is self-propagating, and it can transmit information that can settle disputes over its ownership. As Salmon states, "The ability to transmit a mark is the criterion that distinguishes causal processes from pseudo-processes, for if the modification represented by the mark is propagated, the process is transmitting its own characteristics. Otherwise, the 'process' is not self-determining, and is not independent of what goes on elsewhere."[9] When he says, "what goes on elsewhere," he is referring to the causal process upon which the pseudo-process is parasitic.

The mark theory of causation derives from the first signal view of the universe and provides us with a framework in which to understand causal relationships. As Salmon further states, "A mark is a modification in a process, and if that modification persists, the mark is transmitted. Modifications in processes occur when they intersect with other processes; if the modifications persist beyond the point of intersection, then the intersection constitutes a causal interaction and the interaction has produced marks that are transmitted."[10] Note his reference to *causal intersection*. A mark is the result of a causal intersection of processes, one of which is a causal process. When a causal process interacts with a pseudo-process, a mark is created but it is not sustained or propagated. When a causal process is marked by another casual process, this mark is propagated or sustained. Readers can now see that we must know more about how two processes intersect. This involves understanding their space-time relationships.

Causal Relevance

We can begin to see why the special theory of relativity holds light, the first signal, in such a privileged position and how it is that to which all else is relative. Imagine an event occurring at some point in space-time. For example, let us speculate that the damaged solar collector on the Hubble telescope was caused by a small piece of space junk. Event, E, is the piece of metal striking the Hubble solar collector at some point in space-time.

Imagine, further, all of the light pulses that converge on E. These light pulses form a cone in such a way that the event, E, is at the point of the cone—the last portion of an ice cream cone eaten. Recall that a complete mathematical cone is like two ice cream cones joined at their points. In other words a mathematical cone has two parts that converge at E. As the light pulses that converge on E pass through the point, E, the other half of the Minkowski cone is formed.

All events that are outside of the light cone just described are clearly separated from E in space, and are said to be *spacelike separated* from E. The point in space-time, E, is in the cone and all other points not in the cone must be separated from E in space. All events that lie within the cone are said to be *timelike separated* from E. Events in the light-source side of the cone are past events relative to E, and all events within the other side of the cone are future events relative to E. Note that this makes time (past, present, and future) relative to the first signal, light.

These relationships can be used to clarify the nature of causation. Two events that are spacelike separated cannot have a causal relationship because for one process to create or produce a mark on another process, the two processes must occupy the same point in space-time at which the mark is created. In other words, two causal processes cannot produce a causal interaction if the two processes are spacelike separated. Causal interaction requires causal intersection. The Minkowski cone shows also that all events that could influence E must lie in the past cone for E, and all events that E can influence must lie in the future light cone.

Causing Learning

The mark theory of causal explanation takes us beyond the epistemic theory of scientific explanation in that we are no longer considering the meaning of statements and their relationships, that is, between data and hypotheses.

> The epistemic conception looks upon the world as a place that exhibits various discoverable regularities, and when these regularities are known, the world can be seen as a dependable environment. We come to count on certain regularities, such as the sequence of seasons, and we can anticipate much that we encounter as time elapses, as we go from place to place, and as we perform certain actions. This way of looking at the world leads naturally to an inferential view of scientific explanation, and Hempel's celebrated 'symmetry thesis' of explanation and prediction. For purposes of inference, it is sufficient to be acquainted with the regularities that obtain in the world; it does not really matter what underlying mechanisms give rise to these regularities.[11]

On this theory, we achieve understanding through a reduction of the total number of phenomena that must be considered. As Michael Friedman claims, "This is the essence of scientific explanation—science increases our understanding of the world by reducing the total number of independent phenomena that we have to accept as ultimate or given. A world with fewer independent phenomena is, other things being equal, more comprehensible than one with more."[12] For Salmon, "the most severe shortcoming of this unification thesis . . . is that it makes no reference to the physical mechanisms responsible for the phenomena that are to be explained."[13] Clearly this leads us into the issue of scientific realism versus van Fraassen's "constructive empiricism."[14]

An example of scientific work that was conducted within the framework of regularities is associationist psychology, especially its perfected form: Skinner's radical behaviorism. Behaviorists did not care about "what underlying mechanism gave rise to the regularities" they discovered and, in fact, were skeptical about talk of intentions and goals and all such nonobservable mental processes. They were concerned only with discovering regularities and showing that the world of behavior was dependable if one knew the basic principles. The law of operant conditioning (behavior that is reinforced becomes more frequent) is a law based on invariant associations and explicitly avoids reference to what Skinner considered mischievous animisms. For behaviorists, thinking, like Hume's causal relations, is both unobservable and unnecessary for science.

I want, however, to focus on the question of explanation and Skinner's reinforcement theory. We observe that the change in tides is related to changes in the moon's position. This highly confirmed law of invariant association can be used by sailors and predictors of hurricane damage, but it is not an explanatory regularity. Indeed, it is an *explanandum* that requires explaining. We did not know why the moon and the tides were associated until Newton presented us with his gravitational theory. Is the law of operant conditioning a relationship like the tides and lunar positioning, that is, one that awaits a theory to explain it? Why do the stimuli enumerated as reinforcers increase the frequency of their associated behavior?

Currently, many behaviorists are more willing to go beyond observable associations and to consider underlying causes of behavior. The so-called cognitive behaviorists work within cognitive science to find accounts of why people do what they do. In studies of pigeons learning which keys to peck to get food, Howard Rachlin reports,

> [Cognitive behaviorists] suppose that when the [light in the] sample [key] disappears it leaves an image, called an *internal representation*, somewhere in the animal's nervous system. As time goes on, this internal representation deteriorates. When the comparison stimuli come on, they are not compared to a sample that is no longer present but to an internal representation of the sample. The delay affects the representation and the representation affects the behavior. The object of the experiment, therefore, is to discover what has happened to the internal representation.[15]

Whether these researchers have the details correct or not, they are operating in a fashion consistent with Salmon's view of science.

> The ontic conception looks upon the world, to a large extent at least, as a black box whose workings we want to understand. Explanation involves laying bare the underlying mechanisms that connect the observable inputs to the observable outputs. We explain events by showing how they fit into a causal nexus. Since there seem to be a small number of fundamental causal mechanisms, and some extremely comprehensive laws that govern them, the ontic conception has as much right as the epistemic conception to take the unification of natural phenomena as a basic aspect of our comprehension of the world. *The unity lies in the pervasiveness of the underlying mechanisms* upon which we depend for explanation. [Emphasis in original][16]

Consider Piaget's views. As Kagan comments, "Piaget uncovered a host of fascinating, hardy phenomena which were under everyone's nose but which few were talented enough to see. Those discoveries—the eight-month-old who suddenly becomes able to retrieve a hidden toy, the egocentric answer of a five-year-old on the mountains test, and the shift at age seven from a nonconserving to a conserving reply to the beakers of water—were so consistent across cultures that they resembled demonstrations in a chemistry lecture hall."[17] A child is shown a ball of modeling clay, which is then flattened into a pancake shape. The child is asked if the amount of clay has changed when it was remolded into the pancake. If a child answers in the negative, then that child is said to have conserved, that is, seen that this characteristic remains invariant under the transformation. At some point, children see that matter is conserved in such transformations.[18] Piaget discovered that children do not learn to conserve matter, weight, and volume at the same time. The conservation of weight occurs before the conservation of volume.

Like the ancient sailors, teachers could use this discovered regularity to help them do their jobs better, but these discoveries are not explanations. Piaget has not given us an explanation of the origins of the process of conserving volume. We still ask why: Why do children conserve matter, weight, and volume in that order; what role does age play in this phenomenon?

Scientific Explanation and Professional Practice

Explanation is central to the adequate conduct of professional practices. Any professional practitioner must diagnose clients' situations or conditions because the selection of the appropriate actions is contingent on such diagnoses.

A diagnosis is the classification of a client case in terms of some taxonomy (a hierarchical categorical system). Some diagnoses may be explanatory and some merely descriptive. If the diagnosis is rooted in an explanatory theory, then we know why this case is the way it is, no matter how improbable. If the diagnosis cannot be explained, then practitioners must select actions believed to be effective because of their association with that categorization. Without an explanation, practitioners must treat symptoms because the causes are unknown and thus untreatable. Professional practice is most warranted when diagnoses are explanatory.

Imagine that the standard theory of scientific explanation is embraced along with its symmetry thesis. For professional practitioners this means that they can only diagnose high probability cases. Professional practice would have the highest warrant or justification when it is engaged with typical cases. The exceptional is unexplainable, less treatable, and actions are taken with less warrant. We can select practices on the basis of correlated evidence, that is, treat symptoms, but we cannot give a satisfactory diagnosis of these improbable cases. Salmon's theory offers us an alternative point of view. If improbable cases can be explained as well as typical cases, then the professional practices aimed at these cases need be no less warranted than any other form of professional practice.

One might accept this result and reason that we are not in a deterministic universe; some things happen by chance and we should be mature enough in our thought to recognize this. Children playing in their home are hit by stray bullets. Shots are fired at drivers on interstate highways. Why was this child shot? Why was that car hit? It is very unlikely from a statistical perspective that this would happen to anyone. This would mean that there is no explanation other than chance.

In the context of professional practices this "bad role of the dice" account of why rare occurrences happen seems less acceptable. After several hundred surgeries of a given type there unexpectedly appears a condition that has not been seen before. Why did this improbable situation occur? This may be a significant question for both research and practice, but until now we have not known how to think about such situations. In this time of statistical inference, statistical explanation was considered but was not well developed until Salmon's analysis of statistical explanation, which includes a review of the paucity of attention given this matter. On Salmon's theory of scientific explanation, improbable events are explainable; this feature of his thesis makes it especially appealing to professional practitioners who frequently are faced with diagnosing the improbable.

Teaching as a Causal Process

The application of Salmon's mark theory of causation to teaching is straight-forward. For teaching to be effective it must not only intersect with a learner but it must enter into a causal interaction with the learner. Learners are causal processes because they can be marked by causal interactions and can propagate such marks. Of course, we learn from processes other than teaching. In general terms, we can learn from any causal process that can produce a mark-generating causal interaction with learners. For example, when we began to ride our bicycles on sidewalks, we found that when two slabs of concrete were in different planes (perhaps marked by tree roots), the least bump occurred when the front wheel of the bicycle was run over the point where the two tilted squares of sidewalk meet at the same level. Thousands of children learn this method every year without its being taught to them.

We should not express the causal interaction in terms of teaching and learning because the term 'learning' can be misleading in that it suggests constant change. When children carve initials into the handle of a baseball bat, they create marks that are propagated by the bat because the bat is a causal process. Referring to the baseball bat as a causal process does not mean that the bat is in the state of change. A child as a student in a classroom is also a causal process, and this does not mean that the child as student is changing. We know that there are biological processes that are changing the nature of the child, but when we think of the child as student we do not know that cognitive change is underway. The child can propagate what has been learned as the bat can propagate the initials, but change in cognition is not constant but eventful.

Where are the marks on the learner process when a learner learns? As naturalists, we recognize that a description of the learner process will come, for the most part, from educational psychology. At our present level of knowledge, the marks that the learner process propagates can be at three different levels: the behavioral, the microscopic, and the molecular. This is suggested in R. M. Restak's statement:

> At the *behavioral* level, we express ideas that originate in our cerebral cortex, through spoken and written language, gesture, and even the thoughtful em-

ployment of silence.

This behavioral activity is reflected on the *microscopic* level, where untold numbers of the brain's two to three hundred billion neurons are activated in intricate patterns that a neuroscientist once whimsically compared to an enhanced loom. Each cell communicates with one thousand to ten thousand other cells, making the total number of possible interactions exceed the number of particles in the known universe. The brain's self-reflection and self-reference continue still deeper, to the *molecular* level of organization.[19]

Note that Restak's levels of research parallel McCauley's levels of analysis in defense of folk psychology from complete reduction to neuroscience (see chapter 3).

When a learner emerges from a causal interaction, a mark may be most observable at the behavioral level, but current neuroscience suggests that this mark may have molecular parallels. The point is that, at present, a description of the mark may be written in three different discourses. In neuroscience there is great interest in examining the relations among these discourses, and many expect that the *definiens* of the terms in psychology and neurobiology will more and more contain terms from biochemistry.

Readers might feel that these theoretical reduction urges are playing too fast and loose with meaning. As philosophers of education, we should have this concern, but we should also be acutely aware that to ignore these relationships can be harmful to children. For example, the timid children described by Kagan are neurologically different from the uninhibited children also studied. Acting on the belief that the only difference between timid and uninhibited children are differences in their personal historical schedules of reinforcement is going to lead to educational malpractice. One cannot use social reinforcement to change the number of receptors in a child's neural tissue, or the amount of norepinephrine (the chemical that blocks background noise and allows one to focus on specific stimuli) in the synapses. We must recognize that we are now at a point in our epistemic development where the relationships between observable behavior and underlying causal processes that explain this behavior are beginning to emerge. Kagan points to development in medicine. "All the infectious diseases were defined initially by their surface symptoms because their pathology was not known. Before we learned that Down's syndrome was due to an extra chromosome, membership in the category was defined only by physical appearance. . . . Today the chromosomal anomaly, which can be seen under a microscope, is a vital part of the definition."[20] One expects that as neuroscientific research moves forward, more and more such examples will appear.

Conceptual Analysis and Cognitive Science

Our discussion of causation provides an example of how it is possible *and* why it is important for us to have a methodology of conceptual analysis capable of drawing meaning from scientific inquiry. As we have seen, philosophers are actively pursuing explanatory accounts of how we learn and relationships among all dimensions of cognitive activity are being explored. How could these efforts help but enlighten our answers to traditional questions such as:

What is reasoning or thinking?
What kind of activities help students become better thinkers?
What is consciousness and (teachers' sense of) attention?
How does the mind-brain acquire and process data?
How important is memory in reasoning?

Furthermore, as neuroscience continues its research, the time will come when questions about how best to modify the DNA will not be merely speculative. Philosophy of education should be a major participant in this discussion. But this will not happen unless philosophy of education rediscovers itself as philosophy.

EPILOGUE

ANALYTIC PHILOSOPHY IGNORED the normative discourse of traditional epistemology and sought to enucleate the norms embedded in language. The methodology of analytic philosophy became suspect when it was shown that its claims about the foundations of science were not supported by historical studies of the growth of scientific knowledge. With analytic philosophy of education in retreat, the epistemological relativists in educational foundations were able to take charge of the foundations literature. While epistemological relativism in educational foundations celebrated the effectiveness of its methodology of struggle, the literature known as "cognitive science" was becoming a major focus within philosophy. For example, the arguments of philosophy of mind were being assimilated by philosophy of science. These issues now comprise the cambium of epistemology, but are largely ignored within the courses and literature of philosophy of education. Consequently, philosophy of education as a field of study has removed itself from the mainstream of philosophic inquiry.

The theories being discussed in contemporary philosophy of science are, as I have tried to show, closely related to Dewey's attempts to free educational thought from the epistemological narrowness of empiricism. If Dewey's arguments are significant for contemporary philosophy of science, they should, at least, be considered by contemporary philosophy of education. But a more serious omission is now evident. Academic philosophers working in cognitive science are very much concerned with the nature of learning and cognitive development. The contemporary cognitive science literature can be interpreted as a further explication of Dewey's views. For example, the growing literature on how a naturalized conception of mind might be achieved reveals the continuity of Dewey's views about cognition and the development of intelligence with contemporary cognitive science. As more and more educationists attempt to find applications of the cognitive science literature in education,[1] the inattentiveness of philosophy of education to the analysis and evaluation of what is involved in these applications will become more conspicuous.[2]

Conceptual analysis, in its rejuvenated form, is an essential tool for philosophy of education. My concern is that if philosophy of education courses view all forms of conceptual analysis as either (a) useless methodological artifacts from the age of empiricism or (b) enemies of utopia-building strategies, then the philosophic analysis of thinking, learning, intelligence, and problem-solving will appear to be outside of the nominal philosophy of education courses and publications. This would be unfortunate for an inquiry that is as old as the arguments of Plato and as contemporary as the arguments of Churchland, Dennett, Fodor, and Searle. Of course, philosophy of education as the inquiry into the concepts related to learning and teaching will continue to flourish. The question is, in the years ahead, will it be found in courses and books that bear its name?

NOTES
BIBLIOGRAPHY
INDEX

NOTES

1. The Reemergence of Pragmatism

1. See, for example, John Bruer, *Schools for Thought* (Cambridge: MIT Press, 1993).

2. Randall Collins, *The Case of the Philosophers' Ring* (New York: Crown Publishers, 1978), p. 15.

3. Larry Laudan, *Beyond Positivism and Relativism* (Boulder: Westview, 1996).

4. Ibid.

5. See P. G. Smith, "What Is Philosophy of Education?" chap. 3 of *Philosophy of Education: Introductory Studies* (New York: Harper & Row, 1965).

6. R. N. Giere, *Explaining Science* (Chicago: University of Chicago Press, 1988).

7. Philip Kitcher, "The Naturalists Return," *Philosophical Review* 101, no. 1 (Jan. 1992): 56.

8. Ibid., p. 114.

9. Ibid., p. 54.

10. Steven Stich, *The Fragmentation of Reason* (Cambridge: MIT Press, 1990), p. 28.

11. Ibid.

12. Thomas Kuhn, *The Structure of Scientific Revolutions* (Chicago: University of Chicago Press, 1962), p. 2.

13. See Ian Hacking, "One Problem of Induction," in I. Lakatos, ed., *The Problem of Inductive Logic* (Amsterdam: North-Holland, 1968), pp. 44–58.

14. John Searle, *The Rediscovery of the Mind* (Cambridge: MIT Press, 1992), p. 204.

15. Ibid., p. 205.

16. Peter McLaren, *Critical Pedagogy and Predatory Culture* (New York: Routledge, 1995).

17. Christine M. Korsgaard, *The Sources of Normativity* (New York: Cambridge University Press, 1996), pp. 92–94.

18. Stanley Cavell, *This New Yet Unapproachable America* (Albuquerque: Living Batch Press, 1989), p. 118.

2. The Empiricistic Conception of A Priori Knowledge

1. Gottlob Frege, *Die Grundlagen der Arithmetik*, 1894; translated as *The Foundations of Arithmetic*, by J. L. Austin (Oxford: Basil Blackwell, 1950). See also Frege, "The Concept of Number," in P. Benacerraf and H. Putnam, eds., *Philosophy of Mathematics* (Englewood Cliffs: Prentice-Hall, 1964).

2. Philip Kitcher, "The Naturalists Return," *Philosophical Review* 101, no. 1 (Jan. 1992): 53–54.

3. Ibid., p. 55.

4. Ludwig Wittgenstein, *Tractatus logico-philosophicus Logisch-philosophische Abhandlung* (London: Routledge & Kegan Paul, 1922), sec. 4.111, p. 41.

5. Ibid., sec. 4.1121. Wittgenstein asked that when he was quoted, the original German be presented along with the English or other language.

6. Actually another step should be included. 'A and not A' should be commuted to get 'not A and A', then the second simplification is done.

7. Modus Ponens is the following argument form:

A implies B
A
_____
Therefore, B

8. Gilbert Ryle, "Introduction," *The Revolution in Philosophy* (London: Macmillan, 1960), p. 5.

9. Raymond Kurzweil, *The Age of Intelligent Machines* (Cambridge: MIT Press, 1990), pp. 223–24.

10. Ibid., p. 231.

11. Ibid.

12. E. Feigenbaum, P. McCorduck, and P. Nii, *The Rise of the Expert Company* (Reading, MA: Addison-Wesley, 1988).

13. Kurzweil, *The Age of Intelligent Machines*, p. 225.

14. Jonas F. Soltis, *An Introduction to the Analysis of Educational Concepts*, 2d ed. (Reading, MA: Addison-Wesley, 1978; 1st ed., 1968), pp. 14–15.

15. Israel Scheffler, "Toward an Analytic Philosophy of Education," *Reason and Teaching* (Indianapolis: Bobbs-Merrill, 1973).

16. Isreal Scheffler, *Conditions of Knowledge: An Introduction to Epistemology and Education* (Glenview, IL: Scott, Foresman, 1965).

17. Ibid., p. 8.

18. Ibid., pp. 11–12.

19. Jerome A. Popp, "Practice and Malpractice in Philosophy of Education," *Educational Studies* 9 (Fall 1978): 275–94.

20. Steven Stich, *The Fragmentation of Reason* (Cambridge: MIT Press, 1990), p. 28. In the following sentence he states, "Another younger tradition in epistemology, tracing to James and Dewey, finds nothing untoward in the suggestion that epistemology is inseparable from science and technology."

21. Edmond Gettier, "Is Justified True Belief Knowledge?" *Analysis* 23 (June 1963): 121–27.

22. Ibid., p. 122. In the quotation given, 'e' in the original is replaced with 'B' and 'd' in the original is replaced with 'A'.

23. Ibid., p. 123.

24. See R. Shope, *The Analysis of Knowing* (Princeton: Princeton University Press, 1983).

25. Stich, *The Fragmentation of Reason*, p. 2.

26. Kitcher, "The Naturalists Return," p. 59.

27. Psychology was reintroduced to epistemology on other grounds. For example, D. Armstrong, *Perception and the Physical World* (London: Routledge & Kegan Paul, 1969).

28. Kitcher, "The Naturalists Return," p. 58.

29. The term 'foundationism' in the expression 'methodological foundationism' does not have the same meaning as 'foundation' in 'educational foundations', which is a misleading expression. See Jerome A. Popp, "On the Autonomy of Educational Inquiry," *Educational Studies* 5 (Winter 1974–75): 197–204.

30. See the essays in P. Benacerraf and Hilary Putnam, eds., *Philosophy of Mathematics* (Englewood Cliffs: Prentice-Hall, 1964).

31. W. V. O. Quine, "Two Dogmas of Empiricism," *From a Logical Point of View* (Cambridge: Harvard University Press, 1953), pp. 20–46.

32. Kitcher, "The Naturalists Return," p. 72.

33. R. N. Giere, *Explaining Science* (Chicago: University of Chicago Press, 1988), p. 32. See also Jerome A. Popp, "Paradigms in Educational Inquiry," *Educational Theory* 25 (Winter 1975): 22–39.

34. Thomas Kuhn, *The Structure of Scientific Revolutions* (Chicago: University of Chicago Press, 1962), p. 9.

35. For a classical discussion of the problems of inductive inference, see Wesley C. Salmon's *Foundations of Scientific Inference* (Pittsburgh: University of Pittsburgh Press, 1970).

36. See Popp, "Paradigms in Educational Inquiry," pp. 22–39. See also Larry Laudan, *Beyond Positivism and Relativism* (Boulder: Westview, 1996).

37. Kuhn, *The Structure of Scientific Revolutions*, p. 2.

38. See I. Scheffler, *Science and Subjectivity* (Indianapolis: Bobbs-Merrill, 1969).

39. Nelson Goodman, *Fact, Fiction, and Forecast* (Indianapolis: Bobbs-Merrill, 1965).

40. Daniel C. Dennett, *Consciousness Explained* (Boston: Little Brown, 1991).

41. Patricia Smith Churchland, *Neurophilosophy: Toward a Unified Science of the Mind-Brain* (Cambridge: MIT Press, 1986), p. 288.

42. Giere, *Explaining Science*, p. 5.

43. John Searle, *The Rediscovery of the Mind* (Cambridge: MIT Press, 1992), pp. 224–25.

44. See Ned Block's "The Computer Model of the Mind," in D. N. Osherson and E. E. Smith, eds., *Thinking: An Invitation to Cognitive Science* (Cambridge: MIT Press, 1990), in which he seeks an analytic *a priori* model of the mind. See also Searle's criticism of Block in *The Rediscovery of the Mind*, chap. 9.

45. Imre Lakatos, "Falsification and the Methodology of Scientific Research Programmes," in I. Lakatos and A. Musgrave, eds., *Criticism and the Growth of Knowledge* (Cambridge: University Press, 1970), p. 179.

46. K. Hahlweg and C. A. Hooker, eds., *Issues in Evolutionary Epistemology* (Albany: State University of New York, 1989).

47. For a discussion of this issue, see Salmon, *Foundations of Scientific Inference*, pp. 160–61.

48. R. N. Giere, "Philosophy of Science Naturalized," *Philosophy of Science* 52 (Sept., 1985): 331–56.

49. Lakatos, "Falsification," p. 179.

50. Salmon, *Foundations of Scientific Inference*, pp. 254–55.

3. How Much Can We Learn from Everyday Talk?

1. Ludwig Wittgenstein, *Philosophical Investigations* (New York: Macmillan Co., 1953).

2. Stanley Cavell, *This New Yet Unapproachable America* (Albuquerque: Living Batch Press, 1989), p. 33. This same completeness of commitment to ordinary language is evidenced in Robert Ennis's book, *Ordinary Logic* (Englewood Cliffs: Prentice-Hall, 1969), p. 5; he suggests that, by using the "ordinary meaning of basic logical terms," we can deal with the "reasoning problems of people in their everyday lives" whether they are housewives, mechanics, or Supreme Court justices.

3. Nelson Goodman, *The Structure of Appearance* (Cambridge: Harvard University Press, 1966), p. 6.

4. See, for example, H. Castenada, "Intentions and Intending," *American Philosophical Quarterly* 8 (1972): 139–49.

5. Cavell, *This New Yet Unapproachable America*, p. 32.

6. Ibid., pp. 32–33.

7. Ibid., p. 54.

8. See Jerome A. Popp, "Philosophical Analysis, Research on Teaching, and Aim-Oriented Empiricism," *Educational Theory* 30 (Fall 1980): 321–34.

9. Cavell, *This New Yet Unapproachable America*, p. 43. I made the point less poetically in, "Philosophical Analysis, Research on Teaching, and Aim-Oriented Empiricism."

10. Paul M. Churchland, *A Neurocomputational Perspective* (Cambridge: MIT Press, 1989); Patricia Smith Churchland, *Neurophilosophy: Toward a Unified Science of the Mind-Brain* (Cambridge: MIT Press, 1986).

11. Patricia Smith Churchland, *Neurophilosophy*, p. 152.

12. Ibid., p. 288.

13. Ibid., p. 299.

14. Ibid., p. 395.

15. Reinders Duit, "Students' Conceptual Framework: Consequences for Learning Science," in S. M. Glyn et al., eds., *The Psychology of Learning Science* (Hillsdale, NJ: Lawrence Erlbaum, 1991).

16. Ibid., p. 288.

17. Ibid., p. 289.

18. Patricia Smith Churchland, *Neurophilosophy*, p. 311.

19. Ibid., p. 309.

20. Ibid., p. 152.

21. Daniel C. Dennett, *Consciousness Explained* (Boston: Little, Brown, 1991), p. 319.

22. See, for example, B. Paul Komisar, "Teaching: Act and Enterprise," in C. J. B. Macmillan and T. W. Nelson, eds., *Concepts of Teaching: Philosophical Essays* (Chicago: Rand McNally, 1968).

23. Paul M. Churchland, "Eliminative Martialism and the Propositional Attitudes," *Journal of Philosophy* 58, no. 2 (Feb., 1981): 82–83.

24. Gilbert Ryle, *The Concept of Mind* (Middlesex, England: Penguin Books, 1963).

25. Robert D. Heslep, "Sensations" (presidential address), *Philosophy of Education 1977: Proceedings of the Philosophy of Education Society*, ed. Ira S. Steinberg (Edwardsville, IL: Studies in Philosophy and Education, 1977), p. 18.

26. Robert E. McCauley, "Epistemology in an Age of Cognitive Science," *Philosophical Psychology* 1, no. 2 (1988): 144.

27. C. J. B. Macmillan and T. W. Nelson, eds., *Concepts of Teaching*. A complete list of the best papers on conceptual analysis can be found in Jonas F. Soltis, *An Introduction to the Analysis of Educational Concepts* (Reading, MA: Addison-Wesley Publishing, 1978).

28. See Arno A. Bellack et al., *The Language of the Classroom* (New York: Teachers College Press, 1966).

29. Macmillan and Nelson, eds., *Concepts of Teaching*, p. 2.

30. See Soltis, *Introduction*.

31. See Peter Achinstein, *Concepts of Science: A Philosophical Analysis* (Baltimore: Johns Hopkins Press, 1968).

32. See Jerome A. Popp, "Definition, Logical Analysis, and Educational Theory," in Brian Crittenden, ed., *Philosophy of Education 1973: Proceedings of the Philosophy of Education Society* (Edwardsville, IL: Studies in Philosophy and Education, 1973), pp. 256–65.

33. Jerome A. Popp, "Studying," in Richard Pratte, ed., *Philosophy of Education 1975: Proceedings of the Philosophy of Education Society* (Edwardsville, IL: Studies in Philosophy and Education, 1975), pp. 174–84.

34. Jerome A. Popp, "Practice and Malpractice in Philosophy of Education," *Educational Studies* 9 (Fall 1978): 275–94.

35. Hilary Putnam, "Why We Can't Eliminate the Normative," *Realism and Reason* (Cambridge: Cambridge University Press, 1983), pp. 145–247, esp. pp. 245–46.

36. Jerome S. Bruner, *Acts of Meaning* (Cambridge: Harvard University Press, 1990), p. 33.

37. Ibid., p. 8.

38. Ibid., p. 33.

39. Ibid., pp. 12–13.

40. Ibid., p. 45.

41. Ibid., p. 44.

42. Ibid., p. 47.

43. Ibid., pp. 49–50.

44. Ibid., p. 52.

45. Cavell, *This New Yet Unapproachable America*, p. 60.

46. Bruner, *Acts of Meaning*, p. 41.

47. Ibid., p. 33.

48. Ibid., p. 35.

49. Philip Kitcher, "The Naturalists Return," *Philosophical Review* 101, no. 1 (Jan. 1992): 72.

50. Robert E. McCauley, "Intertheoretic Relations and the Future of Psychology," *Philosophy of Science* 53 (1986): 179–99, and "Epistemology in an Age of Cognitive Science," *Philosophical Psychology* 1, no. 2 (1988): 143–52.

51. McCauley, "Epistemology," p. 149.

52. Ibid., p. 149.

53. Ibid.

54. Ibid., p. 150.

55. Kitcher, "The Naturalists Return," p. 76.

56. R. N. Giere, "Philosophy of Science Naturalized," *Philosophy of Science* 52 (Sept. 1985): 331–56.

57. H. M. Collins, "Stages in the Empirical Program of Relativism," *Social Studies of Science* 11 (1981): 3.

58. K. D. Korr-Cetina, *Science Observed* (Hollywood: Sage Publications, 1983).

59. Peter Berger and Thomas Luckmann, *The Social Construction of Reality* (New York: Doubleday, 1966).

60. R. N. Giere, *Explaining Science* (Chicago: University of Chicago Press, 1988), p. 58.

61. See ibid., p. 131 and citations.

62. Ibid., pp. 131–32.

63. Ibid., p. 132.

64. See Larry Laudan, *Beyond Positivism and Relativism* (Boulder: Westview, 1996), chap. 10.

4. The Pragmatic A Priori

1. See Patricia Kitcher, *Kant's Transcendental Psychology* (New York: Oxford University Press, 1990).

2. Wesley C. Salmon, "Foundations of Scientific Inference," in R. G. Colodny, ed., *Mind and Cosmos* (Pittsburgh: University of Pittsburgh Press, 1968), p. 171.

3. Jean Piaget, *Insights and Illusions of Philosophy*, trans. Wolfe Mays (New York: Meridian Books, 1971), and Konrad Lorenz, *Evolution and Modification of Behavior* (Chicago: University of Chicago Press, 1965), especially the two arguments against behaviorism in chaps. 3 and 4.

4. Lorenz, *Evolution and Modification*, p. 44.

5. Jean Piaget, *Biology and Knowledge: An Essay on the Relations Between Organic Regulations and Cognitive Processes*, trans. Beatrix Walsh (Chicago: University of Chicago Press, 1971), p. 180.

6. J. S. Mill, *A System of Logic* (London: Longman, 1843).

7. A. J. Ayer, *Language, Truth and Logic* (New York: Dover, 1946), pp. 71–87.

8. Salmon, "Foundations of Scientific Inference," p. 172.

9. Thomas Green is willing to embrace the idea (*Activities of Teaching* [New York: McGraw-Hill, 1971]). R. S. Peters used a type of Kantian argument in his *Ethics and Education* (London: Unwin-Hyman, 1966), one of the better, but largely ignored, books in philosophy of education.

10. See Lawrence Kohlberg and Rochelle Mayer, "Development as the Aim of Education," *Harvard Educational Review* 42, no. 4 (1972): 449–96.

11. See Salmon, "Foundations of Scientific Inference."

12. John Dewey, *Essays in Experimental Logic* (Chicago: University of Chicago Press, 1916), pp. 137–38.

13. This was Philip G. Smith's point in *Philosophy of Education* (New York: Harper & Row, 1965), chap. 5, "What Is Science?"

14. See *The Middle Works of John Dewey, 1899–1924*, ed. Jo Ann Boydston, vol. 9: *Democracy and Education* (Carbondale: Southern Illinois University Press, 1980), chap. 7, sec. 1.

15. David Denby, *Great Books* (New York: Simon & Schuster, 1996).

16. John Austin, *How To Do Things with Words* Cambridge: Harvard University Press, 1966).

17. *The Later Works of John Dewey, 1925–1953*, ed. Jo Ann Boydston, vol. 13 (Southern Illinois University Press, 1988), p. 231. Originally published as *Theory of Valuation.*

18. Jerome A. Popp, "Definition, Logical Analysis, and Educational Theory," in Brian Crittenden, ed., *Philosophy of Education 1973: Proceedings of the Philosophy of Education Society* (Edwardsville, IL: Studies in Philosophy and Education, 1973), pp. 256–65; "Practice and Malpractice in Philosophy of Education," *Educational Studies* 9 (Fall 1978): 275–94; "Paradigms in Educational Inquiry," *Educational Theory* 25 (Winter 1975): 22–39; "Aim-Oriented Empiricism and Educational Research," *Educational Theory* 30 (Fall 1980): 321–34.

19. Steven Stich, *The Fragmentation of Reason* (Cambridge: MIT Press, 1990), p. 25.

20. Ibid.

21. R. N. Giere, "Philosophy of Science Naturalized," *Philosophy of Science* 52 (Sept. 1985): 331–56.

22. R. N. Giere, *Explaining Science* (Chicago: University of Chicago Press, 1988), p. 59.

23. Ibid., p. 4.

24. Ibid., p. 5.

25. Ibid., p. 16.

26. Stich, *The Fragmentation of Reason*, p. 149.

27. See I. Lakatos, "Falsification and the Methodology of Scientific Research Programmes," *Criticism and the Growth of Knowledge* (Cambridge: Cambridge University Press, 1970).

28. Larry Laudan, *Beyond Positivism and Relativism* (Boulder: Westview, 1996), p. 127.

29. Salmon, "Foundations of Scientific Inference."

30. Larry Laudan, *Science and Values* (Berkeley: University of California Press, 1984), p. 62.

31. Giere, "Philosophy of Science Naturalized," p. 336.

32. Ibid., p. 338.

33. Ibid., p. 337.

34. Laudan, *Beyond Positivism and Relativism*, p. 134.

35. Ibid., p. 135.

36. C. S. Peirce, *Collected Papers* (Cambridge: Harvard University Press, 1960), vol. 7, paragraph 315, and vol. 8, paragraph 191.

37. Larry Laudan, *Progress and Its Problems* (Berkeley: University of California Press, 1977), p. 138.

38. Philip Kitcher, "The Naturalists Return," *Philosophical Review* 101, no. 1 (Jan., 1992): 69, note 48.

39. Laudan, *Science and Values*, p. 40.

40. Jerome Kagan, *Galen's Prophecy* (New York: Basic Books, 1994).

41. Ibid., p. 7.

42. Ibid., p. 33.

43. Hilary Putnam, *Pragmatism* (Cambridge: Harvard University Press, 1995), p. 69.

5. The Structure of Concepts

1. Peter Achinstein, *Concepts of Science* (Baltimore: Johns Hopkins Press, 1968), p. 4.

2. R. N. Giere, "The Cognitive Structure of Scientific Theories," *Philosophy of Science* 61 (1994): 276–96.

3. E. Rosch, "Natural Categories," *Cognitive Psychology* 4: 328–50; "On the Internal Structure of Perceptual and Semantic Categories," in T. E. Moore, ed., *Cognitive Development and the Acquisition of Language* (New York: Academic Press, 1973), pp. 111–44; "Principles of Categorization," in E. Rosch and B. B. Lloyd, eds., *Cognition and Categorization* (Hillsdale: Lawrence Erlbaum, 1978), pp. 27–48.

4. Rosch, "On the Internal Structure of Perceptual and Semantic Categories." Her data and charts are quoted in Giere, "The Cognitive Structure of Scientific Theories."

5. See references in notes 3 and 4.

6. Achinstein, *Concepts*, p. 6.

7. Paul M. Churchland, *The Engine of Reason, the Seat of the Soul* (Cambridge: MIT Press, 1995).

8. N. R. Hanson, *Patterns of Meaning* (Cambridge: Cambridge University Press, 1958).

9. Giere, "The Cognitive Structure of Scientific Theories," p. 294.

10. Ibid., p. 282.

11. Ibid., p. 283.

12. Ibid., p. 283.

13. G. Lakoff, *Women, Fire, and Dangerous Things: What Categories Reveal about the Mind* (Chicago: University of Chicago Press, 1987).

14. This discussion ignores vertical levels or levels of conceptual abstraction. See Giere, "The Cognitive Structure of Scientific Theories."

15. Ibid., p. 292.

16. Joan N. Steiner, *A Comparative Study of the Educational Stances of Madeline Hunter and James Britton* (Urbana, IL: National Council of Teachers of English, 1993), esp. p. 83.

17. See Robert McCrum et al., *The Story of English* (New York: Penguin Books, 1986), for many examples.

6. Normative Inquiry

1. *The Later Works of John Dewey, 1925–1953*, ed. Jo Ann Boydston, vol. 13 (Carbondale: Southern Illinois University Press), p. 219. Originally published as *Theory of Valuation*.

2. Jonathan Harrison, "Ethical Naturalism," *Encyclopedia of Philosophy* (1967).

3. See Jerome A. Popp, "Practice and Malpractice in Philosophy of Education," *Educational Studies* 9 (Fall 1978): 275–94.

4. Abraham Kaplan, *The Conduct of Inquiry* (San Francisco, Chandler Publishing Co., 1964), chap. 1, sec. 1.

5. Paul M. Churchland, *A Neurocomputational Perspective* (Cambridge: MIT Press, 1989), p. 10.

6. Dewey, *Later Works* 13: 219.

7. Hilary Putnam, *Realism with a Human Face* (Cambridge: Harvard University Press, 1990), p. 25; emphasis in original.

8. Carl G. Hempel, "Valuation and Objectivity in Science," in R. S. Cohen and L. Laudan, eds., *Physics, Philosophy and Psychoanalysis* (Boston: D. Reidel, 1983), pp. 73–100, esp pp. 75, 93.

9. Ibid., pp. 91, 93.

10. Larry Laudan, *Science and Values* (Berkeley: University of California Press, 1984), pp. 63–64.

11. Harvey Seigel, "What Is the Question Concerning the Rationality of Science?" *Philosophy of Science* 52 (Dec. 1985): 517–37.

12. R. N. Giere, *Explaining Science* (Chicago: University of Chicago Press, 1988), p. 10.

13. Dewey, *Later Works* 13: 42–43.

14. Laudan, *Science and Values*, p. 49.

15. Dewey, *Later Works* 13: 25.

16. Ibid., 13: 231.

17. Laudan, *Science and Values*, p. 64.

18. Ibid., p. 63.

19. Larry Laudan, *Beyond Positivism and Relativism* (Boulder: Westview, 1996).

20. Dewey, *Later Works* 13: 229.

21. Giere, *Explaining Science*, p. 275.

22. See Robert Wright, *The Moral Animal* (New York: Pantheon Books, 1994) for an excellent account of evolutionary psychology applied to Darwin himself. D. C. Dennett's book, *Darwin's Dangerous Idea: Evolution and the Meaning of Life* (New York: Simon & Schuster, 1995) is an important philosophic analysis of evolution and cognitive processes.

23. Paul M. Churchland, *A Neurocomputational Perspective*, p. 150. See also Kenneth R. Livingston, "The Neurocomputational Mind Meets Normative Epistemology," *Philosophical Psychology* 9, no. 1 (1996): 33–59.

24. Wallace was actually a co-discoverer of evolution. See Wright, *The Moral Animal*.

25. Laudan, *Science and Values*, p. 47.

26. Giere, *Explaining Science*, p. 44.

27. Paul M. Churchland, *A Neurocomputational Perspective*, p. 147.

28. Dewey, *Later Works* 13: 230.

29. See Laudan, "Shifting Aims and Scientific Progress," *Science and Values*, pp. 64–66.

30. Robert Westbrook, *John Dewey and American Democracy* (Ithaca: Cornell University Press, 1993), pp. 417–18.

31. Albrecht Wellmer, *The Persistence of Modernity* (Cambridge: MIT Press, 1991), pp. 85–86.

32. Ibid., p. 63.

33. *The Middle Works of John Dewey, 1899–1924*, ed. Jo Ann Boydston, vol. 9: *Democracy and Education* (Carbondale: Southern Illinois University Press, 1980), p. 88.

34. Zhores A. Medvedev, *The Rise and Fall of T. D. Lysenko*, trans. I. M. Learner (New York: Columbia University Press, 1969), p. 22.

35. Ibid., 8.

36. Ibid., p. 192.

37. Ibid., p. 192.

38. Zbigniew Brzezinski, *The Grand Failure* (New York: Charles Scribner's Sons, 1989).

39. Ibid., p. 117.

40. Dewey, *Middle Works* 9: 88–89.

41. Ibid., 9: 89–90.

42. Tina Rosenberg, *The Haunted Land* (New York: Random House, 1995), p. 406.

7. Is Teaching a Causal Process?

1. Bertrand Russell, *Mysticism and Logic* (New York: W. W. Norton, 1929), p. 180.

2. Philip G. Smith, *Philosophy of Education: Introductory Studies* (New York: Harper & Row, 1965), chap. 5.

3. David Hume, *An Inquiry Concerning Human Understanding* (Indianapolis: Bobbs-Merrill, 1955), pp. 186–87.

4. Wesley C. Salmon, *Scientific Explanation and the Causal Structure of the World* (Princeton: Princeton University Press, 1984).

5. Carl G. Hempel and Paul Oppenheim, "Studies in the Logic of Explanation," *Philosophy of Science* 15 (1948): 135–74. Reprinted in Hempel's *Aspects of Scientific Explanation and Other Essays in the Philosophy of Science* (New York: Free Press, 1965).

6. Salmon, *Scientific Explanation*, p. 277.

7. Ibid., p. 141.

8. Ibid., p. 139.

9. Ibid., p. 145.

10. Ibid., p. 170.

11. Ibid., p. 276.

12. Michael Friedman, "Explanation and Scientific Understanding," *Journal of Philosophy* 71 (1974): 15.

13. Salmon, *Scientific Explanation*, pp. 259–60.

14. See ibid., pp. 229–38.

15. Howard Rachlin, *Introduction to Modern Behaviorism* (New York: W. H. Freeman and Co., 1991), p. 202.

16. Salmon, *Scientific Explanation*.

17. Jerome Kagan, *Unstable Ideas* (Cambridge: Harvard Press, 1989), p. 91.

18. J. H. Flavell, *The Developmental Psychology of Jean Piaget* (Princeton, NJ: Van Nostrand, 1963), p. 299.

19. R. M. Restak, *Receptors* (New York: Bantam Books, 1993), p. 30. Emphasis in original.

20. Jerome Kagan, *Galen's Prophecy* (New York: Basic Books, 1994).

Epilogue

1. For example, John Bruer, *Schools for Thought* (Cambridge: MIT Press, 1993), seeks to revise the curriculum on the basis of the digital computer view of cognition. Fodor and Dennett have made this view center-stage in the literature. Runate and Geoffrey Caine's, *Making Connections* (New York: Addison-Wesley, 1991) looks at education through the neuro-network view of congition, a view associated with the philosophic writings of Patricia and Paul Churchland.

2. See Jerome A. Popp, "The Role of Cognitive Science in Philosophy of Education," in Michael Oliker, ed., *Proceedings of the Midwest Philosophy of Education Society*, 1998.

BIBLIOGRAPHY

Achinstein, Peter. *Concepts of Science.* Baltimore: Johns Hopkins Press, 1968.

Austin, John. *How to Do Things with Words.* Cambridge: Harvard University Press, 1966.

Ayer, A. J. *Language, Truth and Logic.* London: Victor Gollancz, 1958.

Bellack, Arno A., et al. *The Language of the Classroom.* New York: Teachers College Press, 1966.

Benacerraf, P., and Hilary Putnam, eds. *Philosophy of Mathematics.* Englewood Cliffs: Prentice-Hall, 1964.

Berger, Peter, and Thomas Luckmann. *The Social Construction of Reality: A Treatise on the Sociology of Knowledge.* New York: Doubleday, 1966.

Block, Ned. "The Computer Model of the Mind." In D. N. Osherson and E. E. Smith, eds., *Thinking: An Invitation to Cognitive Science.* Cambridge: MIT Press, 1990.

Bruer, John. *Schools for Thought.* Cambridge: MIT Press, 1993.

Bruner, Jerome S. *Acts of Meaning.* Cambridge: Harvard University Press, 1990.

Brzezinski, Zbigniew. *The Grand Failure.* New York: Charles Scribner's Sons, 1989.

Caine, Runate, and Geoffrey Caine. *Making Connections.* New York: Addison-Wesley, 1991.

Castenada, H. "Intentions and Intending." *American Philosophical Quarterly* 8 (1972): 139–49.

Cavell, Stanley. *This New Yet Unapproachable America.* Albuquerque: Living Batch Press, 1989.

Churchland, Patricia Smith. *Neurophilosophy: Toward a Unified Science of the Mind-Brain.* Cambridge: MIT Press, 1986.

Churchland, Paul M. "Eliminative Martialism and the Propositional Attitudes." *Journal of Philosophy* 58, no. 2, 82–83.

———. *The Engine of Reason, the Seat of the Soul.* Cambridge: MIT Press, 1995.

———. *A Neurocomputational Perspective.* Cambridge: MIT Press, 1989.

———. "Some Reductive Strategies in Cognitive Neurobiology." *Mind* 95: 279–309.

Collins, H. M. "Stages in the Empirical Program of Relativism." *Social Studies of Science* 11 (1981): 3–10.

Collins, Randall. *The Case of the Philosopher's Ring.* New York: Crown Publishers, 1978.

Denby, David. *Great Books.* New York: Simon & Schuster, 1996.

Dennett, D. C. *Consciousness Explained.* Boston: Little Brown, 1991.

———. *Darwin's Dangerous Idea: Evolution and the Meaning of Life.* New York: Simon & Schuster, 1995.

Dewey, John. *Essays in Experimental Logic.* Chicago: University of Chicago Press, 1916.

———. *The Later Works of John Dewey, 1925–1953.* Ed. Jo Ann Boydston. Carbondale: Southern Illinois University Press, 1981–90.

———. *The Middle Works of John Dewey, 1899–1924.* Ed. Jo Ann Boydston. Carbondale: Southern Illinois University Press, 1976–83.

Duit, Reinders. "Student's Conceptual Framework: Consequences for Learning Science." In S. M. Glyn et al., eds., *The Psychology of Learning Science.* Hillsdale, NJ: Lawrence Erlbaum, 1991.

Ennis, Robert. *Ordinary Logic.* Englewood Cliffs: Prentice-Hall, 1969.

Feigenbaum, E., P. McCorduck, and P. Nii. *The Rise of the Expert Company.* Reading, MA: Addison-Wesley, 1988.

Flavell, J. H. *The Developmental Psychology of Jean Piaget.* Princeton, NJ: Van Nostrand, 1963.

Frege, G. "The Concept of Number." In P. Benacerraf and H. Putnam, eds., *Philosophy of Mathematics.* Englewood Cliffs: Prentice-Hall, 1964.

———. *The Foundations of Arithmetic (Die Grundlagen der Arithmetik).* Translated by J. L. Austin. Oxford: Basil Blackwell, 1950.

Friedman, Michael. "Explanation and Scientific Understanding." *Journal of Philosophy* 71 (1974): 5–19.

Gettier, Edmond. "Is Justified True Belief Knowledge?" *Analysis* 23 (June 1963): 121–27.

Giere, Ronald N. "The Cognitive Structure of Scientific Theories." *Philosophy of Science* 61 (1994): 276–96.

———. *Explaining Science.* Chicago: University of Chicago Press, 1988.

———. "Philosophy of Science Naturalized." *Philosophy of Science* 52 (1985): 331–56.

Goodman, Nelson. *Fact, Fiction, and Forecast.* Indianapolis: Bobbs-Merrill, 1965.

———. *The Structure of Appearance.* Cambridge: Harvard University Press, 1966.

Green, Thomas. *Activities of Teaching.* New York: McGraw-Hill, 1971.

Hacking, Ian. "One Problem of Induction." In I. Lakatos, ed., *The Problem of Inductive Logic,* pp. 44–58. Amsterdam: North-Holland, 1968.

Hahlweg, K., and C. A. Hooker, eds. *Issues in Evolutionary Epistemology.* Albany: State University of New York, 1989.

Hanson, N. R. *Patterns of Meaning.* Cambridge: Cambridge University Press, 1958.

Harrison, Jonathan. "Ethical Naturalism." *Encyclopedia of Philosophy.* New York: Macmillan and Free Press, 1967.

Hempel, Carl G. *Aspects of Scientific Explanation and Other Essays in the Philosophy of Science.* New York: Free Press, 1965.

———. "Valuation and Objectivity in Science." In R. S. Cohen and L. Laudan, eds., *Physics, Philosophy and Psychoanalysis,* pp. 73–100. Boston: D. Reidel, 1979.

Hempel, Carl G., and Paul Oppenheim. "Studies in the Logic of Explanation." *Philosophy of Science* 15 (1948): 135–75.

Heslep, Robert D. "Sensations" (presidential address). In Ira S. Steinberg, ed., *Philosophy of Education 1977: Proceedings of the Philosophy of Education Society.* Edwardsville, IL: Studies in Philosophy and Education, 1977.

Hume, David. *An Inquiry Concerning Human Understanding.* Indianapolis: Bobbs-Merrill, 1955.

Kagan, Jerome. *Galen's Prophecy*. New York: Basic Books, 1994.

———. *Unstable Ideas*. Cambridge: Harvard Press, 1989.

Kaplan, Abraham. *The Conduct of Inquiry*. San Francisco: Chandler Publishing, 1964.

Kitcher, Patricia. *Kant's Transcendental Psychology*. New York: Oxford University Press, 1990.

Kitcher, Philip. "The Naturalists Return." *Philosophical Review* 101, no. 1 (Jan., 1992): 53–114.

Kohlberg, Lawrence, and Rochelle Mayer. "Development as the Aim of Education." *Harvard Educational Review* 42, no. 1 (1972): 440–96.

Komisar, B. Paul. "Teaching: Act and Enterprise." In C. J. B. Macmillan and T. W. Nelson, eds., *Concepts of Teaching: Philosophical Essays*. Chicago: Rand McNally, 1968.

Korr-Cetina, K. D. *Science Observed*. Hollywood: Sage Publications, 1983.

Korsgaard, Christine M. *The Sources of Normativity*. New York: Cambridge University Press, 1996.

Kuhn, Thomas. *The Structure of Scientific Revolutions*. Chicago: University of Chicago Press, 1962.

Kurzweil, Raymond. *The Age of Intelligent Machines*. Cambridge: MIT Press, 1990.

Lakatos, Imre. "Falsification and the Methodology of Scientific Research Programmes." In I. Lakatos and A. Musgrave, eds., *Criticism and the Growth of Knowledge*. Cambridge: University Press, 1970.

Lakoff, George. *Women, Fire, and Dangerous Things: What Categories Reveal about the Mind*. Chicago: University of Chicago Press, 1987.

Laudan, Larry. *Beyond Positivism and Relativism*. Boulder: Westview, 1996.

———. *Progress and Its Problems*. Berkeley: University of California Press, 1977.

———. *Science and Values*. Berkeley: University of California Press, 1984.

Livingston, Kenneth R. "The Neurocomputational Mind Meets Normative Epistemology." *Philosophical Psychology* 9, no. 1 (1996): 33–59.

Lorenz, Konrad. *Evolution and Modification of Behavior*. Chicago: University of Chicago Press, 1965.

Macmillan, C. J. B., and T. W. Nelson, eds. *Concepts of Teaching: Philosophical Essays*. Chicago: Rand McNally, 1968.

McCauley, Robert E. "Epistemology in an Age of Cognitive Science." *Philosophical Psychology* 1, no. 2 (1988): 143–52.

———. "Intertheoretic Relations and the Future of Psychology." *Philosophy of Science* 53 (1986): 179–99.

McCrum, Robert, et al. *The Story of English*. New York: Penguin Books, 1986.

McLaren, Peter. *Critical Pedagogy and Predatory Culture*. New York: Routledge, 1995.

Medvedev, Zhores. *The Rise and Fall of T. D. Lysenko*. Translated by I. M. Learner. New York: Columbia University Press, 1969.

Mill, J. S. *A System of Logic*. London: Longman, 1843.

Peirce, C. S. *Collected Papers*. Cambridge: Harvard University Press, 1960.

Peters, R. S. *Ethics and Education*. London: Unwin-Hyman, 1966.

Piaget, Jean. *Biology and Knowledge: An Essay on the Relations Between Organic Regulations and Cognitive Processes*. Translated by Beatrix Walsh. Chicago: University of Chicago Press, 1971.

———. *Insights and Illusions of Philosophy*. New York: Meridian Books, 1971; original French, 1965.

Popp, Jerome A. "Aim-Oriented Empiricism and Educational Research." *Educational Theory* 30 (Fall 1980): 321–34.

———. "Definition, Logical Analysis, and Educational Theory." In Brian Crittenden, ed., *Philosophy of Education 1973: Proceedings of the Philosophy of Education Society*, pp. 256–65. Edwardsville, IL: Studies in Philosophy and Education, 1973.

———. "On the Autonomy of Educational Inquiry." *Educational Studies* 5 (Winter 1974–75): 197–204.

———. "Paradigms in Educational Inquiry." *Educational Theory* 25 (Winter 1976): 22–39.

———. "Philosophical Analysis, Research on Teaching, and Aim-Oriented Empiricism." *Educational Theory* 30 (Fall 1980): 312–34.

———. "Philosophy of Education and the Education of Teachers." In Mary Anne Raywid, ed., *Philosophy of Education 1972: Proceedings of the Philosophy of Education Society*, pp. Edwardsville, IL: Studies in Philosophy and Education, 1972.

———. "Practice and Malpractice in Philosophy of Education." *Educational Studies* 9 (Fall 1978): 275–94.

———. "The Role of Cognitive Science in Philosophy of Education." In Michael Oliker, ed., *Proceedings of the Midwest Philosophy of Education Society*. 1998.

———. "Studying." In Richard Pratte, ed., *Philosophy of Education 1975: Proceedings of the Philosophy of Education Society*, pp. 174–84. Edwardsville, IL: Studies in Philosophy and Education, 1975.

Putnam, Hilary. *Pragmatism*. Cambridge: Harvard University Press, 1995.

———. *Realism and Reason*. Cambridge: Cambridge University Press, 1983.

———. *Realism with a Human Face*. Cambridge: Harvard University Press, 1990.

Quine, W. V. O. "Two Dogmas of Empiricism." *From a Logical Point of View*. Cambridge: Harvard University Press, 1953.

Rachlin, Howard. *Introduction to Modern Behaviorism*. New York: W. H. Freeman, 1991.

Restak, R. M. *Receptors*. New York: Bantam Books, 1993.

Rosch, E. "Natural Categories." *Cognitive Psychology* 4: 328–50.

———. "On the Internal Structure of Perceptual and Semantic Categories." In T. E. Moore, ed., *Cognitive Development and the Acquisition of Language*. New York: Academic Press, 1973.

———. "Principles of Categorization." In E. Rosch and B. B. Lloyd, eds., *Cognition and Categorization*. Hillsdale, NJ: Lawrence Erlbaum, 1978.

Rosenberg, Tina. *The Haunted Land*. New York: Random House, 1995.

Ryle, Gilbert. *The Concept of Mind*. Middlesex, England: Penguin Books, 1963.

———. "Introduction." *The Revolution in Philosophy*. London: Macmillan, 1960.

Russell, Bertrand. *Mysticism and Logic*. New York: W. W. Norton, 1929.

Salmon, Wesley C. "Foundations of Scientific Inference." In R. G. Colodny, ed., *Mind and Cosmos*, pp. 135–275. Pittsburgh: University of Pittsburgh Press, 1968.

———. *Foundations of Scientific Inference*. Pittsburgh: University of Pittsburgh Press, 1970.

————. *Scientific Explanation and the Causal Structure of the World*. Princeton: Princeton University Press, 1984.

Scheffler, I. *Conditions of Knowledge: An Introduction to Epistemology and Education*. Glenview, IL: Scott, Foresman, 1965.

————. *Reason and Teaching*. Indianapolis: Bobbs-Merrill, 1973.

————. *Science and Subjectivity*. Indianapolis: Bobbs-Merrill, 1969.

Searle, John. *The Rediscovery of the Mind*. Cambridge: MIT Press, 1992.

Seigel, Harvey. "What Is the Question Concerning the Rationality of Science?" *Philosophy of Science* 52 (Dec., 1985): 517–37.

Shope, R. *The Analysis of Knowing*. Princeton: Princeton University Press, 1983.

Smith, P. G. *Philosophy of Education: Introductory Studies*. New York: Harper & Row, 1965.

Soltis, Jonas F. *An Introduction to the Analysis of Educational Concepts*. 2d ed. Reading, MA: Addison-Wesley, 1978; 1st ed., 1968.

Steiner, Joan N. *A Comparative Study of the Educational Stances of Madeline Hunter and James Britton*. Urbana, IL: National Council of Teachers of English, 1993.

Stich, Steven. *The Fragmentation of Reason*. Cambridge: MIT Press, 1990.

Wellmer, Albrecht. *The Persistence of Modernity*. Cambridge: MIT Press, 1991.

Westbrook, Robert. *John Dewey and American Democracy*. Ithaca: Cornell University Press, 1993.

Wittgenstein, Ludwig. *Philosophical Investigations*. New York: Macmillan, 1953.

————. *Tractatus logico-philosophicus Logisch-philosophische Abhandlung*. London: Routledge & Kegan Paul, 1922.

Wright, Robert. *The Moral Animal*. New York: Pantheon Books, 1994.

INDEX

Jerome A. Popp is a professor of education at Southern Illinois University at Edwardsville, where he teaches educational psychology and educational research methodology. He has published essays in leading educational journals.